Go Get Benjamin

Reconciliation and Healing

Apostle William O. Epps Jr.

Order this book online at www.trafford.com
or email orders@trafford.com

Most Trafford titles are also available at major online book retailers.

Print information available on the last page.

ISBN: 978-1-4120-5740-0 (sc)

Library of Congress Control Number: 2011905490

Trafford rev. 10/23/2020

www.trafford.com
North America & international
toll-free: 844-688-6899 (USA & Canada)
fax: 812 355 4082

TABLE OF CONTENTS

Go Get Benjamin
Gen. 42:34

INTRODUCTION

In recent weeks it has been the stirring of the Spirit of God in my heart to see a vast harvest of souls into the Kingdom of God. We began to get wind of the Spirit of God's desire while praying in our daily noonday prayer, in the church where I Pastor. During a time of pressing out in the Spirit; we begin to hear prophetically a word, which came forth from the intercessors; a travail for the birthing of souls into the kingdom of God. It was a word that spoke not only to the area and regional concerns of our ministry, but also, to the national and international need for the harvest of men and women into the Kingdom of God. As I begin to preach this word in recent Sundays; I found a greater stirring in the Word to give light and further understanding to the call of the Spirit of God. This revelation in parallel truth, I believe will help to point the way to the time and season that God has established for this great harvest. To that extent, I wish to discuss some truth that I believe will help cause the body of Christ, to be launched into a gathering of a great harvest of souls into the kingdom.

With this then, we pick up in the book of Genesis with the casting of Joseph the son of Jacob into a pit by his brothers: who have become jealous over Joseph and the relationship he maintains with his father. Further Joseph has the promise of God in dreams that he will rule over his brethren. In Genesis 37:5- 11;

"And Joseph dreamed a dream, and he told it his brethren: and they hated him yet the more. And he said unto them, hear, I pray you, this dream which I have dreamed: For, behold, we were binding sheaves in the field, and, lo, my sheaf arose, and also stood upright; and behold, your sheaves stood round about, and made obeisance to my sheaf. And his brethren said to him, shalt thou indeed reign over us? Or shalt thou indeed have dominion over us?

And they hated him yet the more for his dreams, and for his words. And he dreamed yet another dream, and told it to his brethren, and said,

''Behold, I have dreamed a dream more; and, behold, the sun and the moon and the eleven stars made obeisance to me.''

and he told it to his father, and to his brethren: and his father rebuked him, and said unto him, What is this dream that thou hast dreamed? Shall I and thy mother and thy brethren indeed come to bow down ourselves to thee to the earth. And his brethren envied him; but his father observed the saying.

Let's now understand what has transpired in the dreams of Joseph and why they are significant in the eyes of his father and brethren. In the first dream Joseph realizes that he will have dominion over his brethren. They are very much frustrated over the notion of Joseph as headship. Joseph is only repeating what he saw in the dream, but those of his family are quite irritated over his dream. Often we find challenges in relationship. Many are particularly found in families and press us and drive us to do and say things which sever ties and divide unions. This is such a challenge and God uses it to save a people and establish a great nation!

CHAPTER ONE

FOR WHOM IT IS PREPARED?
(Joseph, hated and rejected)

Joseph is to be a type of savior, and his life has been earmarked by God for purpose. That purpose would see not only Joseph become great, but preserve the status of a fledgling nation in it's infancy, that would become great in Jacob. This is the nation of Israel. This move of God to bring His will into fullness is fraught with much struggle. It is the struggle of divine purpose in the lives of His people. It is not at it's initial inception recognized, nor is it readily acceptable to those whom God desired to preserve and establish in the earth with great authority and privilege. God had given dreams to Joseph regarding the desire of God that should come. Because of these dreams; Joseph is hated by his brethren. They become bitter towards him and cast him into a pit. Joseph the dreamer and prophet of God is set upon by them that are closest to him. They not only hate the prophetic anointing of God which is in Joseph's life, but they also despise the fact that his father loved him more than all them. Gen. 37:3 With this, Jacob made Joseph a coat of many colors. It was to show the favor of Jacob toward Joseph. Joseph unquestionably, is special to his father and this is a great irritation to his brothers. Often times in the Body of Christ there is much bitterness and strife. This happens because of envy and jealousy over gifts and positions. It is for those whom God would raise up, not according to that which men can determine according to their own will. It is that, which God himself has said as the final authority for our living. It is that, which is born out in us of the very character of Christ. Much has been squandered of the privilege of the Church because of jealousies and strife, not understanding the heart of the Father. Joseph's brothers did not understand the heart of Jacob and his love for the son of his old age. Often, it's strenuous in the body of Christ because of the failure to understand the will of the Father; and that his desire must be accomplished. When we observe further in this 37th chapter, we can see some patterns of relationship, which develop. Let us start with Reuben the eldest brother who, suggests that they can cast Joseph in a pit: this with the intent of delivering him later from his brothers. This in the onset appears to be a noble gesture. It is however, a copout. Reuben as the eldest son, has the responsibility for making decisions in the absence of his father. He can make the decision that would save Joseph from the hands of his brothers and deliver him back to his father unharmed. Yet, Reuben compromises with them rather than preventing them from not just harming Joseph, but doing anything to remove him from his father. A parallel for this is visible in the body of Christ. It is the failure of those in leadership to take authority for what God has given them. It has caused a serious lack of dominion and power because of disobedience and compromise. Over the years I have suffered many times for keeping the standard of God as my focus. It is an area of great concern in the Body of Christ. The desire of the Father's heart and His will should be at the forefront of our concerns in the things of Christ. God has called men according to the election and calling of Christ, to be responsible for speaking the truth as well as carrying the true expression of His word living in us. There have been compromises for the sake of money and prestige. There have been compromises with the teachings and doctrines of men as substituted for the precepts of Christ. These things have happened for the sake of men having preeminence over the lives of others as well as, hatred of righteousness. (They are afraid to offend). Now, it is worthwhile to note that before he is cast into the pit by his brethren, he is first striped of his coat of many colors. This symbol of his father's love and authority is taken from him. The body of Christ is full of anointed men and women who are called as dreamers and visionaries to the body of Christ and to the world.

And it shall come to pass afterward, that I will pour out my Spirit upon all flesh; and your sons and daughters shall prophesy, and your old men shall dreams dreams and your young men shall see visions.? Joel 2:28

It is because of the jealousies of their brethren that they are not released into their gifting and callings and purpose. Now we do not say that there aren't times of training and equipping these visionaries and dreamers for the purposes of the Kingdom of God and that growth and development are not important. On the contrary, we must develop them and send them forth to do the whole will of Christ. As a spiritual father; i should not be intimidated and jealous our my sons and daughters or evien my brothers in Christ! Yet in Genesis 37:26, we see Judah having a willingness to sell his brother to slavery rather than to deliver him from the hands of his brethren. This too is a heart felt difficulty in the Church. Many who are sick and in the bondage's of sin and brokenness, are left to suffer. They suffer because of the unwillingness of many with gifting and calling in Christ, to stand and declare healing and deliverance to them. Judah does not know who he is initially. This stubbornness and insensitivity to the heart of Christ for his sons and daughters, has left many captive to their circumstances. Jesus was very direct in the acknowledging of his ministry. In Luke 4:18; He declared;

'"The Spirit of the Lord God is upon me, because he hath anointed me to preach the gospel to the poor; he hath sent me to heal the brokenhearted, to preach deliverance to the captive, and recovering of sight to the blind, to set at liberty them that are bruised."

This is the call and mandate of the living God for all those to whom he has given the mantle of ministry, particularly the fivefold ministry gifting. There then, is the need to recognize that we cannot change the mandate of scripture. Further, these mandates have been set according to the dispensational relevance of the time they were given. Therefore, there is nothing that can be removed from the authority of the dispensation. Everything that is stated as part of the dispensation must be completed before it can change. In this we see a parallel truth; That there has been a severe reluctance to acknowledge the five- fold ministry calling and authority of God in the earth. The Church has operated in three- fold anointing for many years and has seen it as all that is ordained of God. Yet, the Word declares the giving of Apostles and Prophets for the perfecting of the body of Christ as well as the Evangelist, Pastor and Teacher. If five- fold ministry is not in operation, the Church cannot be perfected. Eph. 4:11- 13 What then is the question that we raise to determine the validity of the five- fold ministry. We ask, has anything changed in this dispensation to show that all things spoken of in the New Covenant have been fulfilled? Has the Church become unified? Has it come into the measure of the stature of Christ? Is the Church perfected? (mature) It is safe to say that we have not come into these things and until we do, we cannot possibly believe or accept that the Church is ready for a change of dispensation. Likewise, the brethren of Joseph did not understand that they were called to operate according to the dispensational truth and purpose of God for that day. It was to be the establishing of a great and mighty nation to receive the oracles of God himself. They were to be his chosen people. It was spoken in Abraham and everything from that time was to bring it into place. Specifically, Genesis 15:13; *?*

And He said unto Abram, Know of a surety that thy seed shall be a stranger in a land that is not theirs, and shall serve them; and they shall afflict them four hundred years, vs. 14; and also, that nation, whom they shall serve, will I judge: and afterward shall they come out with great substance.?

God is saying to the body of Christ in this hour, that there must be the fulfilling of the whole will of God in this dispensation before anything can change. Our next thoughts begin to take shape in Genesis chapter 42, where we see Jacob as the patriarch and for all intent and purposes; a type of the Church. We say this with the understanding, that in Jacob are all the promises and blessings of God for Israel both spiritual and natural. In similar fashion, we note that the Church has the promises and blessings of God for all mankind. We can see the heart and mind of God for Jacob and the promises that have been given to Abraham. Jacob must now send his sons to Egypt to acquire grain during a great famine and dearth in the land. (Gen. 42:1- 2) Let us note that Egypt in the forefront is a place of abundance and blessing. Yet, we know that as is true with all that is of the world; it brings eventual bondage and death. However, at this point we find blessing and salvation, for those who have no hope; and Joseph becomes then, a type of savior or Christ. We start our discourse with the onset of famine throughout the world and the need for the nations to seek grain in Egypt. Now, Jacob is reluctant to send all his sons to Egypt and he withholds

Benjamin his youngest son. At this time, let us divert from the initial thought and establish that there is a breach, which has existed in the relationship of Joseph and his brethren. This breach in the context of Israel as a type of the Church is essential to understanding the call of God now in the earth. This is the place where we begin to understand, that in order for the purposes of God to come forth in the Church; the Church must be initialized in the Spirit of Reconciliation. II Cor. 5:18- 19 gives us an understanding of God's heart in this hour;

"And all things are of God, who hath reconciled us to himself by Jesus Christ, and hath given to us the ministry of reconciliation; vs. 19; To wit, that God was in Christ, reconciling the world unto himself not imputing their trespasses unto them; and hath committed unto us the word of reconciliation."

The very heart of the Lord in this hour for the Church is the reconciliation of his people. While this is a parallel truth and all truth can be reconciled in the Word of the Lord; Benjamin represents that part of the body of Christ, which is yet to be received into the Kingdom of God. Even though we cannot now talk of them from the vantage point of relationship with the Father in the truest sense. (We speak now prophetically of that which is to be fulfilled). By the prophetic standard of the Lord, (*speaking those things which are not as though they were)*

Ro 4:17;("As it is written, I have made thee a father of many nations,) before him whom he believed, even God, who quickens the dead, and calls those things which be not as though they were" **Rom 4:17b**

they belong to God and there is a mandate of the Spirit to bring them into full relationship. They are with the Father in calling and purpose, to be born out in this absolute end time. Therefore, they must be brought in and established fully with him. They must be sought out by Judah. Judah is the true Church and cannot fulfill it's purpose without the reconciling of the whole body. It is Judah which becomes surety in the presence of their father Jacob to return Benjamin. This then, is become a twofold ministry. The first is the need for men to come into relationships of faith in the living God. The second is a relationship of healing and reconciliation of families and communities and nations in Him. Jacob allows all the brethren of Joseph to go to Egypt except Benjamin.

("For he said, Lest some calamity befall him.") Gen. 42:46

Since Jacob believed that his son Joseph had been lost; he felt that the death or loss of Benjamin would be more than he could live with. He thought that he would shelter his son from the possibility of being lost to him. Such is yet the way of the Church. We have become afraid of losing our children. We are afraid not because of the existence of a vicious adversary, Satan; but because we have not the strength to trust them to the purpose of Christ. This I believe is born out in our unwillingness to correct them or to chasten them. We are become afraid to deal with them and the issues, which, result in their lives because of the worlds condition. (SIN) When we are not willing to speak the truth to them in love and hold them to the higher standard of righteousness; and not the worlds standard: we see and demonstrate a type of hypocrisy which destroys the moral authority which God gave to parents in training up a child in the way that he should go. I recognized this when my son was 13 1/2 years old and he was getting into trouble in school and I thought that I would try to talk to him about the things he was doing without correcting the behavior with strong discipline. I did not realize that there was a need to enforce the standard of truth in his life. I thought that I was being hard on him because I didn't have the courage to correct him in the manner necessary to break the stubbornness and rebellion that was operating. My son at that age was 6'2" at that time and he felt that he was a man because of his size and I was being influenced by his size in believing that he was more mature than his age suggested. Many times we feel that we have the solution to our issues based in what we see without recognizing that there are spiritual forces at work in those issues we face and that they must be challenged with the wisdom of the Holy Spirit of God and His word. After going to the Word of God and inquiring for wisdom; the Lord told me to beat him, he would not die.

Pr 23:14; "Thou shalt beat him with the rod, and shalt deliver his soul from hell".

This was 2 years after I began to have these issues with him. Much of the time we prolong our warfare and the struggle of our condition because we try to apply everything to those issues except the Word of Truth. After I dealt with him according to the Word of God; I never had any trouble with him again. Proper discipline and correction of our children is the central reason for the breakdown in families. Parents do not discipline according to the truth of God's Word. The same is indicative of what has taken place in the Body of Christ where we should have spiritual Fathers that we are submitted to. It is an authority, which, is best served through our obedience to the rule and mandate of Christ as a fit example. Therefore, our priority is that of faithfulness to the Word of God by example and by proper instruction to our children. This is the first aspect of reconciliation in the Church; to win our families. Without the Spirit of Reconciliation there is calamity in the Body Of Christ. There can never be the full purpose of God without the body of Christ walking in the love of God that brings healing and restoration to broken and lost lives. There is now, a great release of the anointing of the Lord to compel souls into the Kingdom of God. We as the servants of the Lord must go to the harvest. That harvest must first begin with our love and concern for the spiritual well-being of our children as the inheritors of the promise of God. The next concern is for those who are within our sphere of influence coming to faith as we pour out the love of Christ upon them. We must go to the harvest.

Jesus told the disciples to: Lu 10:2 *Therefore said he unto them, The harvest truly is great, but the labourers are few: pray ye therefore the Lord of the harvest, that he would send forth labourers into his harvest.*
We must begin to see what God desires and focus on His will for us as well as His Body.

Now Benjamin is the brother who is missing from the relationship of reconciliation with his brothers and Joseph. Joseph is the son whom God has sent into Egypt to prepare the way for his brethren to be sustained in the time of famine and hardship. This is the hour when God has raised up many to be a Joseph in the bringing of lives into balance and peace with God. There is a tremendous witness of the men and women of God, who have had to endure much hardship and brokenness. They were broken in order

to be used by God to deliver and set free many captive souls, in obedience to the call of the Spirit of God in their lives. The Word of God tells us the certainty of this grace given to The Body of Christ in;

2Co 1:4 Who comforteth us in all our tribulation, that we may be able to comfort them which are in any trouble, by the comfort wherewith we ourselves are comforted of God.

Christ is preparing the Church to sustain the world and reveal the wisdom of God in this end time. It will not and cannot be done without the reconciliation of the body. The second aspect of this is the generations which are before us. There are currently two generations separated from the purposes of God. The first is one of great importance to the end- time work of Christ in the earth. These, are Benjamin. They are a young and radical people with a tremendous sense of fairness and have become very bitter against the established norms of society. They are acute in their judgments of society and the Church World. (they that profess Christ and godliness) They do not want to be controlled in the status quo of the Church and are rebellious to the hypocrisy that they have seen. They are hungry for a new experience and relationship with God. Yet they need the word of salvation and the reconciliation that comes through forgiveness and healing. It is the Christ kind of love and mercies which will break every yoke and release them into their purposes in the Body of Christ. This, with a willingness to allow the Holy Spirit to move and change the heart and ideas of the Church away from tradition and men's opinion, can bring the fullness of Christ alive in the body. The second is the generation that is currently being born, from zero to 10 years of age, which cannot come into his inheritance and walk out fully his destiny until the Church begins to display its love: first a love for one another and then for them, which are lost. Only then, will it allow a renewing of the kindred Spirit of God; to heal and deliver from the wounds of the past. At this season of harvest, God is calling the Church to be fully and completely reconciled. God allowed great dearth in the land so that there would be of necessity, a stirring of hearts to go into Egypt and seek grain to live. Yet, there lives would not only be saved by natural substance, but by spiritual recourse: (the need to repent and gain forgiveness). There is also the necessity of Christ, laid upon us one and all: it is the need to not only confess to one another, but to bow before one another and serve our brethren. The brothers of Joseph had sent him into exile and slavery, because God gave him a dream in which they; his brethren, realized they would be subservient to him. Gen. 37:3 points out the fact that they were jealous over him because of his relationship with their father.

"Now, Israel loved Joseph more than all his children, because he was the son of his old age."

Also, he made him a tunic of many colors, which showed that Joseph possessed the favor of his father. It is difficult at times for men to receive from other men, because they are jealous over the favor of God in their lives.

Vs. 4; "but when his brothers saw that their father loved him more than all his brothers, they hated him and could not speak peaceably to him. "

It is a condition of the body of Christ where we will not receive one another's authority because we are jealous over the anointing. There is a difficulty in the Body of Christ in that, there is a change that is taking place. It is the change between two Orders with the passing of the mantle of authority from the Old Prophetic Order to the New Apostolic/ Prophetic Order. The first Order has been overrun with the mixing of the Word of God with the commandments of men. It is a legalism and type of judaistic rule in the things of God. It has been restricting of the grace and liberty of the Lord, by the will of men and a moving away from the Spirit and intent of God. In this we see an unwillingness to change or a hesitation, to allow for the move of the Spirit of God that brings change. Joseph by operating in the prophetic anointing and gifting, saw that God was raising him up to have dominion. He was to be the leader and provider of salvation to his family and everyone around him. It was a part of the divine order and course of God.

There are many things to be discussed when we consider that God is a God of continual change and diversity. Sometimes, in the mind of men; there is the belief that change will somehow diminish the greatness of God or subvert his authority. It is for all concerned, the fear that men have of losing control which is the first problem. When we operate by the leading and direction of the Spirit of God; we begin to see another type of authority and power demonstrated in the body of Christ. It is the fundamental purpose of the Holy Spirit to lead and guide the people of the Lord into all truth. This is made clear to us in Jn. 16:13a.;

"Nevertheless, when he, the Spirit of Truth is come, he will guide you into all truth."

Note: It is the job of the Holy Spirit to bring the Father's will to fullness in the people of God. In the training and equipping of God's people, it is certain that the Holy Spirit will bring the Body of Christ of age and into full maturity before the Living God. The Word tells us that the spirit of agreement brings the release of power. It is primary for God to desire unity and agreement in bringing the power of God to deliver and set free the people of God. These two ingredients then are necessary to the making of the people of God complete. Unity brings a place of oneness and must be confirmed through our ability to agree together as one heart. When men can agree together and unite in their efforts and position; God will release the power. Why then should we have a need for the power of God to be demonstrated when the Word tells us that God has already given us power over all the power of the enemy. It is clear that even though the Word of God speaks of the power that He has given. It is not in operation the way that it should be in the Body of Christ. For this very reason; no unity and no agreement, NO POWER! When we agree together and become united as one in heart and purpose, the power is given. It is then, the power that demonstrates the authority that He has given to the Church. Invariably, it is given to men in order to be born out in the collective and corporate body of Christ. The key to this type of authority is the humility and meekness of those who would lead. Jesus told his disciples in Matthew 20:25- 28;

"You know that he that rules of the gentiles, lords it over them, and those who are great exercise authority over them. Vs. 26, yet, it shall not be so among you; but whoever desires to become great among you, let him be your servant. Vs. 27, and whoever desires to be first among you. Let him be your slave- Vs. 28, Just as the Son of Man did not come to be served, but to serve, and to give his life a ransom for many."

In order to have the true authority and power we must have the same spirit that Jesus had. Men are consumed by whatever lords over them. Pride and arrogance have been a great thorn in the hearts and the will of many, who use the disguise of service to God. It is the motivation of the heart that God see's and is concerned with. The brothers of Joseph were concerned, that this, their younger brother should rule over them and that he would receive the birthright of his father, even though he was a younger son. To rule in their culture; was to possess the privilege of the eldest son. This would be totally unacceptable in the mind and hearts of his brethren. For this reason and the fact that their father loved Joseph; they hated him. Yet, God held a better plan and purpose for Joseph and for the sons of Israel. (Jacob) This is not unlike the concern of the disciples who were concerned with who would have the high place in the Kingdom of God. Jesus said in Matthew 20:23b;

"but to sit on my right hand, and on my left, is not mine to give, but it shall be given to them for whom it is prepared by my Father."

No man can walk out the destiny which is prepared for another man. Oftentimes, it would seem that men have tried, to not only build for themselves kingdoms of this world and thrones; but also, that they would even dare to intrude into the purpose of God with blatant disobedience and force by, refusing to give up to His heart and desire. They have done this in order to keep to themselves in position and authority over God's people.

Yet, Revelation 11:15b tells us;

"the kingdoms of this world are become the kingdoms of our Lord and of his Christ; and he shall reign forever and ever."

No matter what men have set up for themselves, they can never take what has been set apart by the word of God for his eternal glory forever. Joseph simply walked out the destiny, which God had purposed for his life. The people of the Lord must advance in the Kingdom of God, by walking out what has been prepared for them from the foundations of the world. Much of the difficulty in the Church world stems from the misalignment that is prevalent in the churches. Poor leadership in following the direction of the Holy Spirit has made chasms of disarray and confusion. These have separated and divided the power and strength of the Church as a corporate body. It is God's heart and will to bring unity and agreement to the body. There must be an alignment; so that the fullness of Christ may be demonstrated in the world. The World must see the manifestation of the Sons of God. It then takes the spirit of unity and agreement to demonstrate it. The strength of agreement in this hour will come through the Apostolic and Prophetic offices of the fivefold ministry coming into authority in the Body of Christ. It is a struggle of the Church in this season to hear the mandate of the Spirit of God, for a release of these offices, to establish the Church in structure and order and new direction. So then, in the second order, there is a new prophetic authority being raised up in the body of Christ. It is an authority that will come through the ones who are humble enough to serve the body of Christ by the example he set in the death of his own son Jesus Christ; it will be carried out in those willing to carry about in their bodies the sufferings of the Lord Jesus. Even as the Apostle Paul stated in Colossians 1:24,

"I now rejoice in my sufferings for you, and fill up in my flesh what is lacking in the afflictions of Christ, for the sake of his body which is the Church."

This is clearly seen in the testimony of Joseph. Joseph held a prophetic promise from God; but he had to walk out the years of suffering and humility. Joseph suffered not only the hatred of his brothers; he also suffered the temptation of Potiphar's wife. NOTE: When there is an anointing in your life and men see the favor of the Lord on you; they will try to corrupt and steal away your blessings (by corrupting your anointing). People, many times are drawn to the anointing in your life and want to control or possess it. We as the Church must guard the anointing. The anointing is an evidence of Gods presence with us. The presence of God was with Joseph. Joseph was cast into prison and still God used him and gave him great favor and blessing in the midst of his struggle to become what God had spoken concerning his life. The Church will always be confronted with struggle and hardship at times; yet, it is not without grace in the midst to propel it past it's circumstances. Because of the prophetic gifting in him, he is yet a blessing to all that would allow the demonstration of God's purpose. Yet, because of the presence of God with him; he is given responsibility, by his captors, in their affairs.

The Church is a place for demonstration of the power of God. It is set in the world to advance the Kingdom of God in the earth. That advancement is not without struggle and warfare. We must be willing to suffer and yet to show the heart of Christ by love and obedience to his will. As Joseph, we are given responsibility for the affairs of mankind in the earth. As he interpreted their dreams and was wounded by their indifference to his needs: so must we reveal the wisdom of the Lord God and become Christ's resolve and open display for all to see in the world. God demonstrates through Joseph his resolve to not only lead his brothers and family; but a nation into the glory of the Lord. Now while there is no doubt that Joseph is tried for his making; God knowing the timing of all things used his life's condition and circumstances to accomplish his will. However, it must be clear to us, that there is nothing in heaven or earth which can divert us from our purpose, when we have settled our heart to walk in him. The hatred and contempt of his brothers could not stop the will of God for Joseph. His brothers hated him and they despised the prophetic revelation of God to him. They and the various conditions, which Joseph came into, could not determine the outcome of his destiny. Nothing in heaven or earth can avert the plan of God for his children when they walk in him with courage and steadfastness. God remains in control and his power and authority is given to them, which are exercised by obedience, to fulfill his will. (HIS WILL FOR YOU IS YOUR PATHWAY TO YOUR DESTINY)!!!!!!!!!!!!!!!!!!!!!! Your condition does not dictate the will of God. Whatever you may have to endure as a matter of living life; you are still on course for the prophetic declaration God has given to you, to be fulfilled. All He requires of you is a faithful and obedient heart. Part of the difficulty of this hour, is jealousy and suspicion which comes from the contrasts between the Old Prophetic Order and the New. It is a refusal to hear and obey the changes, which the Holy God is commanding. This with a further resistance, to the Apostolic heart of the Lord being released into the Body of Christ; is a resistance to the call for greater order and structure in the Church. It is not a legalistic attitude regarding dress and codes which have nothing to do with holiness; but it is an actual call to right thinking with right actions. How do we regard our neighbor and what is our behavior toward them? God is calling into question the intent of the heart and the motivations by which we operate. Jesus told the multitudes in Matthew 5:21- 28; that the intent of the heart was the main concern of God by his witness to them in his instruction. In Vs.21- 22, he told them about the misunderstanding of the word concerning death and judgment. He informs them further that, to be angry with a brother without a cause, puts them in danger of the judgment. To judge and condemn another was to be in danger of hell fire. In the next two verses; Christ exposes them to the Father's heart by showing them how to approach the throne with their sacrifices. God the Father desires our reconciliation and then our sacrifice. When we have violated the civil code and are called to give account; The Lord instructs us to agree first. This is an act of confession and if we are unwilling to confess; then we are forced to pay the penalty of the law. Then, in the last verses, 27- 28; Jesus exposes the very need to regulate our thoughts and desires: to guard against lust and protect ourselves from even the thought of sin. He tells them that to look on a woman and desire after her is sin. When you know in your heart, that if you had an opportunity to do what was wrong morally, you would do it: whether by action or by fantasy; it is sin. There are many in spiritual dilemma because of the idols they worship in their hearts by lustful thoughts and wicked imaginations. Yet, God is clear in his purpose regarding the intent of the heart and our need to have a clean spirit before him.

CHAPTER TWO

HE WHOM GOD HATH SENT
Gen. 37:12

In Genesis 37:13; Joseph is sent by his father to see his brethren and to inquire as to their well- being in Shechem. In the course of carrying out the instruction of his father; Joseph begins to wander. Often, we are given the mandate of the Father and told to go forth, still we wander. We know our instruction but not how to perform it. But, there is a man who sees Joseph wandering and asks him where he is going. The God of all righteousness has someone prepared to assist you in the times of your wanderings. God will use others that are called to purpose, to help you stay on course with the call of Christ in your life. The body of Christ is anointed to the purpose of God. In that purpose, it is predisposed to care for the brethren. We are to heal and strengthen one another. We by the leading of the Holy Spirit; care for and protect the people of faith. We cover and serve and do whatever is the mandate of the Word of God for our lives. We see then part of the trouble in the body. Not everyone is willing to receive you in your charge. Vs. 18

"And when they saw him afar off, they conspired against him to slay him."

You are called and set forth to be a blessing in the earth, but not everyone in the Church world is happy about your calling. Vs.19;

"They said to one another, behold, this dreamer cometh."

Whatever the gifting and calling of the Lord in your life; your greatest opposition will come generally from your family: both natural family and your spiritual family. As the people of the Lord, we must allow for the trial and persecution which comes with being chosen for His purpose. Joseph is plotted against and we do not speak of the plotting as a reason for alarm. It is merely a point made to bring understanding that we cannot expect to inherit the kingdom blessings without opposition from the prince of this world. Part of that opposition will come from men, ie. family members being influenced and used by him. Joseph is thrown into a pit by his brothers, who have determined to kill him. There is some intervention on the part of Reuben who is not willing to allow his blood to be shed. While on the surface this may appear noble on the part of Reuben; it is a cowardly act because he does not have the heart of his father. Reuben in the 49 chapter th of Genesis is the first to receive the prophetic blessing of his father Jacob before Jacob dies. Jacob tells Reuben; Vs. 3- 4;

"Reuben, thou are my first- born, my strength, the excellency of dignity, and the excellency of power. Unstable as water, thou shalt not excel, because thou wentest up to thy father's bed; then defiledst thou it: he went up to my couch."

Reuben has the potential to become a great man of God and to inherit the authority of his father. He cannot inherit it because in going up to his father's couch he demonstrates the weakness of his flesh and the thinking of the natural man. That weakness is an attempt on his part to rule, not as a man of the Spirit but of the flesh. You cannot rule in the affairs of the Living God through your senses and emotions. Rom. 8:6a

"The carnal mind is enmity against God."

Reuben has the typical mentality of the church world. It is a spirit of duality and a mixture of gifting with false morality. *(That, which looks and sounds holy, but underneath is infested with sin.)* Jesus in his confrontation with the religious order of his day, tells them; *Matt.23:27;*

"Woe unto you, scribes and Pharisees, hypocrites! For ye are like whited sepulchers, which indeed appear beautiful outward, but are within full of dead men?s bones, and of all uncleaness."

It is not merely an appearance of righteousness that our God is interested in. It is actual holiness and godliness in living which excites Him. That Holiness and Godliness in living is who he is in us. Because of this, we cannot expect gifting to be the focus or emphasis of righteousness. Rom. 11:29; states:

'For the gift and calling of God, is without repentance.''

The gifting is given by God to enhance that in you, which is set forth to be the evidence of God's character in the earth. We are the representation of Christ in the world and our gifting is to bring his power and blessing with the revelation of his presence. This is the very reason why Adonijah the brother of Solomon is put to death. He supposes that to possess the kingdom, he must have the concubine of his father David. He proceeds by asking Solomon's mother, Bathsheba to intercede for him with Solomon. His request is for Abishag the Shunamite in marriage. He believes that if he possessed her; who had been his father David's concubine; he could possess the kingdom of David. He knew that the inheritor of the kingdom possessed all that pertained to his father and by possessing his concubines he could take the kingdom from Solomon. 1 Kings 2:13- 25 Please note, that it is the destiny of Joseph before the Lord, to walk in the purpose or God. It is such for every individual who will do the will of the Lord. Yet, we are able to abort our true destinies by our actions and denial of His purpose for us. It was not the will of God for Adonijah to inherit the throne of his father David. Even though Adonijah had purposed in his heart to take by deception and trickery what did not belong to him. Such is the case, in many instances in the Church World: a desire to build thrones and kingdoms in the place of Christ's purpose and throne. *(You cannot walk out another man's purpose and destiny in the earth.)* During the ten days of the disciples, after the ascension of Jesus; they decided while in the upper room waiting for the promise of the Father to hold a meeting. This meeting was to determine who it was, that should take the place of Judas Iscariot as Apostle. They cast lots and received one Matthias, who was numbered with the apostles. Acts 1:20- 25 NOTE: We cannot use fleshly or natural things to determine spiritual things. The purposes of God in Christ are not subject to the will of the flesh. Now, even though Matthias is chosen, we have to consider by the scripture; that it is the Apostle Paul that is chosen by the Lord to take this Apostleship. It is he that is chosen to bring the message of salvation to the gentiles. Paul himself says in: I Cor. 15:8;

"And last of all he was seen of me also, as of one born out of due time."

We know that there is a grace that is extended to us at times because of the desire to do a good work. That desire however, does not supercede God's purpose and will. For example: Paul writes to Timothy and explains the qualifications for the office of overseer. A If a man desire the office of bishop, he desireth a good work. Yet, understand that, there are only five ministerial callings in the body of Christ. Ephesians 4:11 declares;

"And he gave some Apostles; and some Prophets; and some Evangelists; and some Pastors and Teachers; vs. 12; for the perfecting of the saints for the work of the ministry, for the edifying of the body of Christ."

There is therefore, a desire for the office of overseer, which is a Pastoral office and yet, the individual does not necessarily possess the ministerial calling to the office of Pastor. There is a mantle which is passed with the authority of the office. It is confirmed in the anointing that is given to carry out the work. Still, God will honor the desire and service of one who has the heart to do the work. We do however contend that the perfect will of God is before every person, and they therefore, must choose to walk it out. You cannot walk out that which is prepared for another. The final thought regarding this, is Christ's statement regarding the mother of James and John. She asks Christ to grant her a request: that her sons sit, one on the right hand and one on the left. Jesus replies that it is given only by the Father and to them for whom it is prepared. Jesus showed further, that there was a work of the Spirit involved with what they asked. He called it a baptism and asked if they could be baptized with his baptism. Every born again believer must realize that they are appointed to the purpose of Christ before the foundations of the world. There then, is the wisdom of the Spirit of God to reveal to each the mystery of that purpose.

The word of God declares that before we entered our mother's womb, He knew us. We then have been assigned to walk out the purpose for which we were intended. Many will abort the purpose of the Father in their lives, because we all have the free will to do as we desire in this life. Yet those who will submit to the will of the Father will know an intimacy with him that goes beyond the limits of the finite mind to reason or understand. Therefore, to be immersed in the plan of the Lord Jesus, is to be baptized according to the will of the Father. Every struggle or difficulty; every hurt and anxiety; every confusion or frustration; commands an expectation for the promised end: and we endure because the one who promised will not allow his word to fall to the earth. He will bring a performance of the things which he says. We cannot abridge the sovereign will of God. What God has prepared for every person is set in eternal wisdom and can only be fulfilled by submission to his will for our lives. With this the Word of God declares, Rom. 1:20;

"for the invisible things of Him from the creation of the world are clearly seen, being understood by the things that are made, even His eternal power and godhead; so that they are without excuse."

God is not going to allow the purpose of Christ to be hidden from those who desire after him. We must seek first the Kingdom of God and His righteousness (all these thing will be added unto us) Mt. 6:33 God will reveal His heart and purpose but only to them that search for Him. Now, Joseph was willing to endure hardship, even as a young man, because he loved the God of his father. He possessed a relationship with him and gave himself to the purpose which was established for him. His brothers did not realize the divine purpose of Jehovah God. So then, they tried to destroy Joseph for his prophetic insight. We note here also, that Joseph is sent to enquire concerning his brethren by his father Jacob, in spite of the fact, that he knows that they hate him. Perhaps, Jacob believed that they would not do anything against him because he was their brother. Nothing could be further from the truth. You and I must know, that even though we are a apostolic and prophetic people, set in the earth in this hour to accomplish Christ's purpose; you are hated in many circles where we should be received. You are a threat to the conformed and traditional attitudes of the Church World. When you follow the Word of the Father; (to go and seek for your brethren);

often there is no desire in many of them to receive you. They will call you dreamers and radicals and fanatics, when your only desire is to do what you have been commanded to do by the Father. In Gen. 37:18- 19;

"And when they saw him afar off, even before he came near unto them, they conspired against him to slay him. And they said one to another, Behold, this dreamer cometh."

There has been a fearfulness, in them who say that they love God, to hear his voice and come into his presence. It is the kind of fear that gripped Israel in Ex.34:33. Moses as the prophet of God has come into the presence of the Lord. He has spent much time seeking the heart of the Father. As a result of this time he has spent with the Lord, he is changed in his appearance. The glow of the Lord is upon his face. His countenance is changed. The people whom Moses has led from Egyptian captivity into the wilderness, and have seen many miracles and know the might and power of the sovereign God; have still, reluctance to hear and receive Moses. They cannot be content with him in leadership, because he is changed. They want the change in him to be hidden from their view. Ex. 34:33

"And till Moses had finished speaking with them, he put a veil on his face."'

This glow on Moses' represents the glory of the Lord to be revealed in man in the earth. Many in the Church World do not want this demonstration, or want the suffering and struggle. We find this born out in Ex.10- 11; that God has again expressed a desire to speak to Israel. The Lord does not merely intend to send a word to his people, but decidedly wants to speak to them, face to face. Yet, before He begins to speak and reveal his heart to them; they move away from his presence and stand afar off. (Chapter 20, vs. 18, 21) There are several keys to these passages of scripture. The *first key* is that they should sanctify themselves and wash their clothes the first two days and then He would speak to them on the third day. There is the need before God through Christ's blood, that men should sanctify themselves and wash themselves. It is the need to come clean with Him and allow him to speak to us His heart. The image of who God is is in his Word. If we as a people are not willing to agree with his Word; we cannot agree with him. The Word of

God cleans and makes new the hearts of men through the blood of Jesus Christ. He gave them the commandments of God. Ex. 20:1- 17 The *second key* is that of, setting our hearts to obey the commandment of the Lord regardless of the circumstances which are before us. When the people saw the thunder and lightening, and the noise of the trumpet, and the mountain smoking; they removed themselves and stood afar off. There are many times when the Spirit of the Lord is calling for a greater intimacy in the people with the Father. The difficulty lies in the fear and unbelief which arises because of the warfare and the conditions of opposition that come. In much of the time it is merely an intimidation and oppression, to keep the real purpose of God from coming forth. Again, in the great commission of Matthew 28:18; we receive the instruction of Jesus Christ regarding the responsibility given to the Church for propagating the Gospel. There are three major concerns to be developed here. Firstly, The Call must be made. All men must know, that the Living God desires a relationship with them. It is the job of all the born again believers in God, to preach and teach the Word of God, to every creature. It must be given without compromise. It cannot be watered down or sugarcoated. It must be spoken with the full intent of the Spirit of God. Secondly, every man (woman, boy, or girl) must believe in their own heart, that there is accountability for what they have heard. In Hebrews chapter 8:10, the writer speaks of the covenant that he will make with the house of Israel. Vs. 10b.;

"I will put my laws into their mind, and write them in their hearts; and they shall be my people. Vs. 11; and they shall not teach every man his neighbor, and every man his brother, saying, know the Lord; for all shall know me, from the least to the greatest. "

Therefore, the word of God cannot be subverted or changed, to suit the whims of them that hear it, neither them that preach it. As God called all Israel to hear Him; He further challenges every man to hear and obey his Word. We are not given the luxury of picking what we will believe and adhere to. All the Word of God is our responsibility and each of us must know Christ for ourselves. This was evident in Joseph. He recognizes he has a responsibility to hear the word of his father and to respond to the command given him. This is true even though, he is not liked or well received by his brethren. His brothers in conspiring against him, to slay him, were incensed at his boldness to speak the prophetic vision of the Lord to them. It is the time, when the people of the Lord must speak the prophetic mandate of the Spirit of God, regardless of the resistance that comes. Men will say, *"Behold this dreamer cometh."* Yet, they themselves will come in time, to the realization, that you are come for their good. There may even be plans devised against the purpose of Christ in you, however; we still must walk out our course. The victory is already set in the purpose of God for your life. You and I must complete the process. (Go through the test). Reuben will come and thwart part of the plan of the enemy against you; (his other brethren wanted to kill him), but it did not keep Joseph from the other areas of suffering in his life.

CHAPTER THREE

STRIPPED OF COVERING
Gen.37:23

And it came to pass, when Joseph was come unto his brethren, that they stripped Joseph out of his coat, his coat of many colors that was on him. Gen. 37:23

It is necessary to note at this point, that Joseph is at the mercy of his ten brothers. He is set upon by them because of their jealousies and envy. They hate the fact that he is loved more by their father than they. They hate his prophetic insight, even his relationship with the Lord God of Israel. Joseph is thrown into a dry pit while they sit down to eat. There are many times in our lives as believers, that we will be placed in a hard place in relationship. Nothing is more difficult than our relationship and dealings with family. Oftentimes it is the very place, where God will test us and reveal many of the challenges of change to be made in us. This is done that we may evolve to a greater level of holiness and relationship with him. The same is true whether in our natural family or our spiritual family. There can be many times in our experience, that we are stripped of that which symbolizes the promise and the blessings of our father. Again, it is not the losing of things or symbols which abort the promises. It is the failure to walk out our destinies through the lack of compliance with the will of Christ. This then will abort our destiny and cut off the promises of God to us. However, for the faithful believer, there can be no defeat of the Words of promise given us by our Father, when we stand and accept His will in our lives. oseph is determined that the will and promise of the Living God will not fail in his life. Joseph gives himself wholeheartedly to serving God regardless of his condition and circumstances. Beloved, Christ desires our determination and commitment to staying the course and allowing HIM to work in us both to will and to do of HIS good pleasure.

Php 2:13; "For it is God which worketh in you both to will and to do of his good pleasure."

His will must become the focus of our living. Joseph has the distinction of proving whether or not he will fulfill the prophetic mandate of God in his life. You must prove out the promise of the Lord through your obedience to him. This is a difficult word for many. The promises and prophecies of Christ are based on our obedience. Many have been aborted by the sin of unbelief or unwillingness to walk obediently.Life oftentimes; will cause you to experience the pit of circumstances, and seem to cause you to be sold to the slavery of conditions beyond your control. In this we see a parallel truth in Eph. 6:8;

"As knowing that whatever good thing any man doeth, the s ame shall he receive of the Lord, whether he be bond of free."

It is how you live out those difficult times, that you realize your growth and potential. Furthermore, Heb. 6:10

"God is not unjust to forget your work and labor of love, which your have shown toward his name, in that ye have ministered to the saints, and do minister."

There is the reward which comes because of our patient obedience to walk out the course which the Lord God has earmarked as our destiny. It is to be carried out with steadfast and heart felt obedience and love for Him, who called us. Joseph is thrown into the pit, and that, after having been stripped of his tunic of many colors. It appears, he while having the favor of his father; is helpless and unable to deliver himself out of the pit. There are many pitfalls to observing the commandment of our Father. The struggles at times may appear to be endless. The oppositions to ministry and the frustrations of ministry can be overwhelming. No doubt, Joseph felt that he was hated without cause. He perhaps believed he was alone and his situation very grievous. This is not unlike many of the circumstances that we face in life. The witness of a true spirit and relationship with our God is the ability to stay in the fight. We cannot allow the pressures of circumstance to force us out of purpose. It is the pressure of what we face that equips us to do an even greater ministry. We must go through the fire of trial in order to come forth in purity of faith. The Word of God shows us this truth in 1 Pe. 1:7; it is the trial of our faith which is more precious than gold that perishes. That trial of faith, many times must endure the fire of the Spirit, in order to bring us aligned with our purpose. No matter the degree of difficulty in our trial, God will always stand with us to deliver us in the full assurtiy of faith. So, our concern then becomes, will we believe Him in the midst of our struggle. The struggle then, that is before Joseph is one of walking out the process of stripping. Let's define the term stripping and study it's impact upon Joseph. Stripping, according to Strong's Concordance is the Hebrew word Pashat meaning to spread out (i.e. deploy in a hostile array): to strip (i.e. unclothe, plunder, flay etc.): fall upon, flay, invade, make an invasion, pull off, put off, make a road, run upon, rush, set, spoil, spread selves (abroad), strip (off, self). This shows us that it is a term of warfare in it's initial state. The brethren of Joseph had conspired to take him and remove him from themselves by first desiring to murder him. They were constrained by Reuben who suggested that they should throw him into the pit.

"Shed no blood, but cast him into the pit that is in the wilderness and lay no hand upon him." Gen. 37:22b.

They had stripped him of the coat which his father Jacob had given to him. This is the act of desperation in his brothers which show their hatred for the place of favor that Joseph maintains with his father. In terms of the spiritual significance of those things which have happened; we find that Joseph as one who is prophetically called by God to carry out a specific purpose; has come to this time of warfare. This warfare is direct evidence in the natural for what is taking place in the Spirit Realm. In the Spirit Realm there is a contending made between the forces of Satan and the Armies of the Lord. The Angelic host of God are fighting according to Hebrews Chapter One and verse 14.

"are they not all ministering spirits sent forth to minister, for them that shall be heirs of salvation."

There is a sad commentary to be made at this point in the book. It is in regard to the carnality of Joseph's brethren in thinking that they could prevent the purpose of Joseph from coming to fruition by removing him from the presence of Jacob. They had spent there time being contentious with Joseph because his father loved him more then them all. Yet, God who is sovereign in all things has scheduled a time for processing Joseph and the struggle is in fact on course with God's purpose. Rom. 8:28

"And you know that all things work together for good to them that love God and for those that are called according to His purpose.")

So, we see both naturally and spiritually a deployment and hostile array against Joseph. Then we note that they unclothed him by pulling off his coat. Another aspect of this unclothing or pulling off of Joseph's coat is that of removing from Joseph the very thing he values most. It is the coat which his father has given him. It is a place of favor and blessing. The coat also signifies the promise of his father as the favorite son and Joseph held great pride because of his possession. *(This is the proof that I am my father's son and have his favor).* When God gives us the possession *(whatever it may be)*; we cannot afford to lose sight of the fact, that God is the blessing and not what he has given us. Again, Joseph is in process. Not only is it important to note that he is in process, but the process is come as a result of the need in his life to learn to not speak what has been revealed by God out of season. The dreams which have been given to him become a source of antagony for his brethren. Joseph being young hasn't the presence of fore- thought to hold what has been revealed by God to him. *(zeal without knowledge)* Partly, he struggles with the prophetic anointing in his life and having a desire to see what God has said come to purpose. Yet, as with all of those who will do His will; we must know His character. God did not show him these things because he wanted Joseph to gloat or lord over his brethren. He showed him to stir Joseph prophetically to be mindful of His calling on his life. Now, when we understand that we have calling and purpose on our lives, we further recognize the need for submission and humility as the method of character God desires in us. The usual struggle for many is the ploy which the enemy uses to remove you from your covering. We must not abort or hinder the maturing process by pride and arrogance because of gifting. Lets try to understand this in terms of covering. Covering is first a place of protection and provision. Joseph should been safe with his brothers. Now, this begs the question. Even though we have many Joseph's in the body of Christ; the need for covering and protection has been diminished through the jealousies and petty squabbles of spiritually immature people. The Spirit of Accusation and the Spirit of Division have brought continual separation and contentions in the Body of Christ. Why have these kinds of problems been allowed to take there toll on the Body of Christ? Why have the Joseph's of our generation been sent to Egypt? Why have the Ishmeelites been allowed to buy our gifted? The body of Christ is now seeing the training and equipping of the Joseph's in places of turmoil and struggle; partly because it has not provided the atmosphere necessary for hearing the heartbeat of God. The brothers of Joseph should have had the heart of their father and showed to Joseph the same favor that Jacob showed. Whether it is right to show favor or not would be challenged by conventional spiritual wisdom. However, we are not speaking of respect of persons which is based on the will of men for personal gain. We are speaking of the desire to do that which blesses another simply because we delight in being a blessing. Why weren't his brethren amenable to being a blessing to this son whom their father loved? The reason for their ambivalence and hatred of Joseph is spiritual. They were worldly and carnal. They hated the righteousness of Joseph. There are many in fact in the body of Christ who hate righteousness and are spiritually defunct in their hearts of the true character of Christ. Joseph loved the God of his Father and stayed true to the dreams that God had given him. The fact is that although the brothers of Joseph were to become a great nation, and a holy nation unto God: they were not holy. They were deceivers, and vengeful. They lived in the lust of the flesh and the pride of life. This is evident in how they murdered the men of Shalem, a Canaanite city because they had defiled their sister. (See Genesis chapter 34) It is evident that they did not possess the love and kindness that was needed to forgive and heal wounds. (unmerited favor) Neither did they possess the grace of their father Jacob. Yet, Joseph lives out love in practice that becomes evident in his reconciliation with his brothers. The next reason for the division is God's call and purpose in bringing Israel into Egypt for the next four hundred years to build a nation to worship the true God. Now, we must know that it did not necessarily mean that this state of affairs were the only means whereby God could bring about the purpose of God for Joseph and Israel. *Rom. 8:28*

"and we know that all things work together for good to them that love God and are the called according to his purpose."

God could have done it another way! God in giving the promise to Abraham has again made a commitment to fulfill the promise which he had given. He watches over his word to perform it. In Genesis 15:13- 14; God tells Abraham,

"know certainly that your descendants will be strangers in a land that is not theirs, and will serve them, and they will afflict them four hundred years. And also, the nation whom they serve I will judge; afterward they shall come out with great possessions."

So we find here the promise of God, which is given to Abraham and is initialized in Joseph and finalized in Moses coming as a deliverer to bring them out of that captivity. This happens as it was spoken by God. In the process of time God was working the end from the beginning. He gave the ending first and then went back to the beginning to bring the appointed end. Whatever has been necessary to establish His will, He what he did. God will use the foolish things to confound the wise. It is not the wisdom of men which will prevail but the wisdom of God.

Let's discuss the Spirit of Accusation and Division. Accusation is the act of accusing or bringing formal charges and allegations against another. It also, makes the person charged guilty of some punishable offense. The Body of Christ is by association and relationship to Jesus Christ guilty of all charges and specifications recognized as a part of the world's hatred of Christ and His Church. In John 17:14; Jesus said, *"have given them thy word; and the world has hated them, because they are not of this world, even as I am not of this world."*

This is further confirmed in 1st John 3:13;

"Marvel not my brethren if the world hate you"

We then are not taken by surprise at accusation and the attempt of the world to divide or destroy the things of Christ. (Understand beloved that Satan is the accuser of the brethren and the world is under his influence). Rev. 12:10b. We are however, very concerned with those things within the Church which divide and separate the brethren. This is a very bad and devouring influence of the Adversary (Satan) in taking every opportunity to neutralize the effectiveness of the Church through division and strife. *1st Peter 5:8 tells us;*

"Be sober, be vigilant; because your adversary the devil as a roaring lion walketh about seeking whom he may devour."

Now, in reference to the Church bringing in or allowing division and separation to operate; it shows in part, a failure to recognize and confront sin with the love and truth of Christ and to set the standard of God by the spirit and intent of HIS heart in our dealings one with another. Part of the division comes by the evil surmising's of men's hearts against one another. This then is a leadership problem of the highest magnitude. Fundamentally, the Church should be against all sin. The Word of God is the absolute rule for our living. If this is not the essence of our relationship with the Living God, the Church will become and in many instances has become like the world in it's heart and spirit; cold and impersonal with no hope of experiencing the glory of the Creator in truth and righteousness and peace. Now I am not talking about becoming legalistic in our administrations of the truth in confronting sin, but the bible says;

Eph 4:15; "But speaking the truth in love, may grow up into him in all things, which is the head, even Christ:"

The sons of Jacob did not have the love of God in their hearts as did their father and part of the workings of God in this issue with their brother Joseph has to do with them being taught to receive the heart and mind of the Father as well as recognizing HIS love for them and the use of Joseph to prepare a way for them and their generations to be blessed.

The sons of Jacob were carnal and did not mind that their brother Joseph was separated from them. They surmised that Joseph was being arrogant and held a blatant disregard for the order of the birthright. Yet, the Word of God vindicates Joseph in showing his ability to work through extreme pressure and maintain the right perspective and heart in every relationship. The major shift in the Spirit has to do with bringing the Church into unity and agreement, not based on what we suspect is the problem or concern but actual legitimate needs. It is an emphasis upon restoring the family as a major cohesive unit in the Body of Christ. Failure to do the Word of God is the paramount reason for the Church failing in its attempt to demonstrate the power of God.

"Again I say unto you, that if two of you shall agree on earth as touching anything that they shall ask, it shall be done for them by my Father, who is in heaven". Mt.16:19

The key here is agreement; both with the Word of God and with one another. We need a demonstration of the presence and power of Christ in the earth. It is the manifestation of the Sons of God that will show the glory of Christ in the earth. Romans 8:19 says:

"For the earnest expectation of the creation waiteth for the manifestation of the sons of God."

This can only happen through the unifying of the body of Christ. The Church must be one heart and one soul and one spirit. The damage of the family of Jacob came from within and not from without. The need of the brothers to remove Joseph from his father's house is a carnal and selfish dismissal of one of their own, taken from under the covering of his father and placed in the hands of the Ishmeelites for profit.

Many have been denied the privilege of relationship and leadership which has vision and insight to help bring their lives into purpose. The brothers are bent on taking Joseph away from his father and such is the way of men who hate vision or purpose that is not their own. The desire of Satan through the use of men's flesh is that of removing those in the Body of Christ with vision and promise; away from God's intended purpose. Joseph is a young man who is given dreams by God for the purpose of later ministry to preserve not just his family but to sustain nations of the earth by the wisdom of God. A further examination of the question of why our gifted have been placed in the hands of the Ishmeelites is our next concern. Joseph as the anointed of the Lord gives us insight into this question. He is sold for money at the suggestion of Judah to the Ishmeelites for twenty pieces of silver. This is the cost of relationship, not only with his brothers but with his father Jacob. We as believers wound and cast out our brothers and sisters for the sake of money and approval and acceptance for the sake of the will of men. The gifted of Christ are placed in pits of despair and hopelessness because we have not accepted the differences of anointing and purpose in their lives. However, the Word of God declares;

"But ye are a chosen generation, a royal priesthood, an holy nation, a peculiar people, that ye should show forth the praises of him who hath called you out of darkness into his marvelous light. Which in times past were not a people but now are the sons of God." 1 Pe.2:9

So then, just as Joseph is gifted and given vision; God has gifted many in the Body of Christ and given them vision. We cannot dismiss them because we do not like what God has done. Romans 9:20; clearly defines our role in understanding the purpose of God in establishing His will in men.

"Nay but, O man , who art thou that repliest against God, shall the thing formed say to Him that formed it? Why hast thou made me thus"?"

We have no right to challenge the wisdom of God. Our heart must align itself with the heart and will of our Father. To dismiss the brethren because we have differences of color and purpose or thinking is to show God as a God of limited ability and vision. Isa. 55:8

"His thoughts are not our thoughts and His ways are not our ways"

Such, is the greatness of the God we serve. We cannot lose the blessedness of diversity and matchless creativity in Christ; as God has given these things for the blessing of the whole Body of Christ. This is can be seen in Revelation 7:9*;*

"After this I beheld, and lo, a great multitude which no man could number, of all nat ions and kindred, and people, and tongues stood before the throne, and before the lamb, clothed with white robes, and palms in their hands."

The present task of the believer is one of restoration and healing in the body. It is also that of allowing the Spirit of God to bring every part of the body into it?s designed purpose and function. You and I would not reject any part of our natural body; even parts which we believe have no comeliness. We would not reject any part because it is our body. We must not reject any part of the Body of Christ because it is His body. Rom. 8:6a

"So we being many, are one body in Christ, and everyone members one of another.? Having then gifts differing according to the grace that is given to us."

God's desire is that of accepting and appreciating the differences within the Body of Christ and allowing the completion of His will for the Church through us.

CHAPTER FOUR

"POTIPHERS HOUSE"
(Gen. 39:1- 23)

We have come to the time now, when Joseph has been sold, to the Captain of The Guard. It is a man by the name of Potipher who purchases Joseph from the Ishmeelites. In this, we also note that the scripture declares that the Lord was with Joseph and that he was a prosperous man in the house of his master in Egypt. The fact that we have come into adverse circumstances does not mean that we cannot be blessed or prosperous in the trial. In chapter 39 of Genesis verse 2; we then understand that there is the condition of slavery and yet the prosperity of the Lord is with Joseph. As believers, there is a grace which is born out of purpose and destiny. It allows for the favor of God and is revealed even in the extremely adverse conditions. Potipher recognized the anointing and glory of God that was with Joseph. There are many times when the unrighteous are tugged upon by the Spirit of God to exert some influence or some authority for the sake of the believer. Yet, let us note that Joseph is also righteous. He is obedient to the things of God. There must be a loyalty and integrity that is commiserate with the character of Christ in us. (We who believe) Our trials are always about the character of God being revealed in us. Potipher is a representative of the world system and order. He is governed by his loyalty to Pharaoh and the system of Egypt. While the world is an unholy place; it is not without spiritual insight. It is classified in the world system of reason as gut instinct or premonition, but is really the working of prophetic ability given by God but corrupted by demonic influence for the purpose of worldly gain. Potipher sees Joseph as an opportunity to advance his personal gain in the system and economy of Egypt. In verse 3 it is noted;

"And his master saw that the Lord was with him and that the Lord made all that he did to prosper in his hand."

Potipher places Joseph over all his household and the Word of God says;

"Joseph found grace in his sight (Potipher's) and he made him overseer over his house and all that he had put into his hand"

Verse 4 Also the Egyptian is blessed for Joseph's sake because of the law of God which is set in Abraham. God told Abraham that he would bless them that blessed him and curse them that cursed him. Gen. 12:3 Joseph is blessed in the promise of Abraham as a holder of the vision and purpose of God to raise up a nation of priests to worship the True and Living God. To bless Joseph is to bless Abraham's seed and to bless Abraham's seed is to bless Abraham, and to bless Abraham is to be blessed of God for Abraham's sake. The body of Christ is placed in the world to bless the world. Our ability to be a blessing is not determined by our circumstances. Our circumstances should an opportunity to bring the glory of God to the world.

Joseph had the Glory of The Lord resting upon him. This is the anointing which The Lord places on the life of individuals for purpose an anointing that brings the order of God for the fulfilling of that purpose. Further he was anointed for the market place and that gifting in his life affected the home and fields of Potipher. The Church has been reluctant to use the anointing that God has given in the market place because of fear and ridicule from men. The Joseph anointing will cause the people of God to effect a change in the market place as well as in private homes. In the Joseph anointing the key is character. Joseph is termed a goodly person which has been interpreted handsome but does give the full perspective of the statement. Gen. 39:6b; *"And Joseph was a goodly person, and well favored."*

One bible source records that he is also a pleasant thing and a precious thing. So we note that there is something in the character of Joseph which makes him very special and is much noticed and drawn upon by Potipher. It should be such in the Body of Christ that we stand out in the anointing and demonstrate a spirit and presence of Christ which affects

everything and everyone we come into contact with. Joseph had such a presence and anointing. So much did Joseph possess this presence and anointing that his master had no knowledge of all that he had except the bread which he ate. Genesis 39:6a Everything that Joseph did, prospered in his hands and he was faithful to his master. When will the people of the Lord be faithful to Him. This is a paramount issue in the Body of Christ. It is the placing of individual purpose and pursuits ahead of God's desire for us. Lets take note here of the fact that you and I as did Joseph do not live without struggle. There is now the occasion of the enemy to bring temptation and testing into Joseph's life. It has become an opportunity for the enemy to bring reproach to the name of God. Joseph is being pursued by Potipher's wife. She is a woman who also recognizes the anointing that is upon Joseph and desires to possess him. It must be noted that many times people will be drawn to the man or of God. They will want to hang around with them and to buy gifts and do many things for them. Often they themselves do not realize for what reason or why they are drawn to the man or women of God. It is the anointing that is on the life of the person that is attractive to them. Even though it is the classic struggle between right and wrong; it is the same work of the enemy that comes against the purposes of Christ in the lives of all believers. The need to resist the devil is made clear in James 4:7;

"Submit yourselves, therefore to God, and resist the devil, and he will flee from you."

The classic struggle for the believer is one of submitting first to God. It is evident that Joseph is living in submission to the will of the Father because he runs out of the grip of Potipher's wife and leaves his garment. Joseph protects his anointing first. The people of God must be willing if necessary to leave even their own identity for the sake of Christ. Joseph's decision is based on a true principle of the scripture that is first to be recognized and understood as the very heart of any issues regarding sin. Joseph refuses to lie with Potipher's wife and asserts that there is no one in the house who is greater than he. He shows that the issue of regard in this struggle is twofold. The first concern is that of his Masters trust. In verse 9a Joseph states that *"there is none greater than I, neither hath he kept back anything from me but thee, because thou art his wife."*

Joseph is respectful and willing to keep covenant with his Master. He is again loyal and integrous to do that which is right concerning another. He then states that it is also a wicked thing. With then his second concern he asks;

"how then can I do this great wickedness, and sin against God?? "

Joseph realizes that every sin is first and foremost a sin against God. Every believer must come to understand that every sin is first and foremost a sin against God. Often there is the regard for whom it will offend when we do these things. But, the primary consideration should never be focused on merely offending individuals but on the offense we bring to Christ. It would have been a reproach to the name the God he served to sin with a blatant disregard for the truth. Further his character is tested in the absence of witnesses. See verse 11. The fact that Joseph runs out of his garment further indicates his desire to please the Father by doing the right thing regardless of who would see or know. God should be able to trust his sons and daughters without reservation to do the right thing. Joseph was that kind of obedient son. God trusted him, even in the testing to do the right thing. Your circumstance does not determine your obedience. Your submission to the Word of God does. Leave your garment in the enemies hand if necessary and run away from the sin. *(Resist the devil and he will flee from you?)* **James 4:7b Some will ask the significance of leaving ones garment as it is stated here in Genesis 39:12. It is the need for men to be totally exposed in there behavior. That is, the willingness to be completely naked before God and man in showing the righteousness of relationship with Christ. Our trial is not so that God can determine what we will do. He already knows. It is to prove to us what we will do under the pressure of testing. It is that we can understand the need to be completely honest with God and ourselves. We must learn to be true and truthful in every area of our living. The later charge against Joseph is that he came to lie with Potipher's wife and to mock him and his household. But Joseph is completely naked and open before Potipher. Potipher knew Joseph's heart**

and Joseph's offense should have been terminal. Yet, Joseph is not killed but placed in prison. Some of the attacks of the enemy are designed to take your life. God however, will only allow that which is necessary to align you with His purpose. We can clearly see that the purpose for the life of Joseph is greater than the struggle which he endured. So it is that the appointed end of that which is determined by God will prevail. *("Who hath known the mind of the Lord that we may instruct him")* I Cor. **2:16a As we** recognize the warfare which is made against Joseph; it is also needful to note that Joseph went from one aspect of warfare which begins with his brethren and is then heightened in the household of Potipher. Curiously, the average Christian believes that there is either no warfare or only a minimal type of warfare. This is born out in the way most perceive not only the kind of struggle they are in but the complaint they make. The continual question in most struggles is how long? Or I must have done something wrong because I seem to have bad luck. They have not understood that, what they wrestle with are spirits and principalities and powers which through ignorance and lack of understanding in the people of God gain advantage over them and bring their defeat. Ephesians 6:12 tells us;

"For we wrestle not against flesh and blood, but against principalities, against powers, against the rulers of the darkness of this world, against spiritual wickedness in high places."

The Body of Christ must believe that there is a war taking place in the heavenlies and that that warfare affects what is taking place in the earth. The impact of the Church must be made first in the Spirit Realm. We as the people of the Living God live principally in the Spirit first and then operate in the earth. But because of the mind set of the carnal man; we operate in the things of the God or attempt to, with the same carnal thinking and behavior as the world. But the Word of God declares that; Rom. 8:7- 8;

"the carnal mind is enmity against God; for it is not subject to the law of God, neither indeed can be. So then they that are in the flesh cannot please God.'

Our obedience to the will of Christ is born out first and foremost through our acceptance of the Word of God as the absolute rule for our living. When we begin to declare the Word in our will and speak it forth; the Spirit Realm becomes impacted by the authority of that Word. Joseph held on to the promises that were given to him by God. He has accepted the Word of God and the absolute rule for his living and in the midst of all opposition he has become fortified in faith. *("Without faith it is impossible to please God.")* **Heb. 11:6**

Now, Joseph is an example of the Obedient to the Word of God and the need to endure through the warfare by prayer and relationship. Joseph held a good relationship with the Father and because of that relationship; he resisted Potipher's wife. He valued that relationship with the Father more than carnal desires which came to tempt him. He is under the constant barrage of Potipher's wife's sexual advances and still he resists the temptation. The carnal mind is a continual place of tempting. Yet, the bible says, I Cor. 10:13;

"there hath no temptation taken you but such as is common to man; but God is faithful, who will not suffer you to be tempted above that ye are able, but will with the temptation, also make a way of escape, that ye may be able to bear it."

Joseph fled and got out. There must be a willingness to flee in the face of temptation by the people of God. *It is about proper character!!!!!!!!!!!!!* It is not about who lied on you; Potipher's wife lied on Joseph. It does not matter that you have been thrown into prison as was the case of Joseph. God expects that you and I will embrace His character. Relationship with Christ is a matter of men being transformed into His image and likeness. Circumstances do not determine your character. Obedience to or lack of obedience to the commandment is the evidence of your character. In this though, we see that while he is placed in prison: Joseph yet receives mercy from the Lord and favor from the keeper of the prison. Gen. 39:22 Note that anything that was done there, Joseph was the doer of it and because the hand of the Lord was with Joseph; the Lord caused him to prosper.

CHAPTER FIVE

'THE FORGOTTEN"

Let us now begin this chapter with the imprisonment of Joseph who has in spite of being charged falsely, is placed in charge of everything that pertains to the keeper of the prison. This also included the placing of the prisoners in Joseph's care. Joseph is the number one inmate. He is given the responsibility of caring for the other inmates. Quite often the greatest testing of your ministry will come during the times of your incarceration. While many of us may not be in a literal jail; because of our circumstances at times it would seem that we are captives in mental prisons and spiritual bondages of trial. It is not always needful to be placed behind bars to know being captive to hurt and brokenness. Still, Joseph is given ministry to do and he must do it regardless of his personal dilemma. Oftentimes the Christian will not stand up and do his or her ministry because they believe that to do ministry you must have ideal conditions. However it is the times when you are at your worst when the Holy Spirit will make demands upon you for ministry. Partially we must recognize that there are in Christ no bad or poor opportunities for ministry. There are no conditions which preclude or negate the call of God which is in an individuals life. Christ was in the midst of his greatest crisis of personal need and suffering when he said to the thief on the cross: Luke 23:43;

''this day shalt thou be with me in paradise.?

Conversely, we cannot do less than Christ himself did. The glory of God rests upon the inadequacies of men who have yielded themselves to the will of God and realize that it is through no strength or ability of there own that these things were done. In this we glorify God.

Joseph is given the opportunity to minister to two individuals among the prison population. Much of the time we are not constrained to meet the needs of other desperate and broken people because we do not have the love of God working in us. Joseph is able to keep his focus because he loves the Father and is willing to do ministry regardless of personal need. The people of the Lord must love Him more than they love themselves. In chapter 40 of Genesis, a divine connection has been made for Joseph. It is a connection which gives Joseph inroads into the Kings palace. While it is not immediately accessible, it is only a matter of time. Joseph is given the chance to minister to the Kings chief butler and chief baker who have been thrown into prison because they have angered the King. Joseph is charged with serving them and they continued a season in prison. Verse 4 Joseph has a need to be served but is pressed upon by the Keeper of the Prison to serve the butler and baker. As we later discover; Joseph is called upon to interpret the dreams of these individuals. He comes into their presence in the morning and finds them sad. How is it that Joseph who is set upon to serve these men is even concerned about their condition. He is not bitter and not woeful or distraught over his personal condition and is able to serve with joy. The condition does not determine our countenance.

Joseph finds out that they have dreamed and has a word of encouragement for them because they are saddened not having an interpreter. While the initial need is to know the meaning and there is frustration on the part of the Chief Butler and the Chief Baker at not knowing: Joseph hast been sent to this place and time for this purpose. Your situation may at times be difficult but you must know that you have come to this place for such a time as this. This is a divine appointment. Many will miss their time of blessings because they have not recognized the need for their condition and position in the place they are in. We are called upon to do ministry without hesitation and to love and be gracious inspite of the trial. Joseph in interpreting the dreams gives good news to the butler and very bad news to the baker. There is much to glean from this passage but we will not endeavor to discuss everything in its content. The simple truth to be examined is that of saying what God is saying regardless of the message to be spoken. Joseph has a very good word for the butler but the word he gives to the baker is bad news and hard to express. Yet, it is necessary to give them the understanding and to trust the living God to handle all the details and necessities of the situation. The difficulty in this is that of wanting to be free of the personal condition which exists with Joseph and he asks the butler in verse 14;

"but think on me when it shall be well with thee, and show kindness unto me, and make mention of me unto Pharaoh, and bring me out of this house."

Joseph like many of us wanted to be out of the prison that he was in and hoped that this time of ministry would bring his release. He began to explain his trouble and the unfairness of his situation. Having been stolen away he says out of the land of the Hebrews;

"and here also, I have done nothing that they should put me into the dungeon."

He feels justified in his argument and appeals to the hearts of men for his freedom. However, God did not place Joseph in this position because of sin in his life. In John chapter nine there is the question which is asked of Jesus concerning a blind regarding sin.

"And his disciples asked him, saying Master, who did sin, this man, or his parents, that he is born blind"

Jesus answered, John 9:2- 3;

"Neither this man sinned, nor his parents, but that the works of God should be manifest in him."

We must remember that God is the sovereign creator and is trying to demonstrate his works in us.

Often we feel that we have been faithful and deserve to be free from the warfare and struggle of our situation. The truth of the matter is that we are not our own and have been purchased with a price. Because we are not our own we forget our focus and commitment is to Christ the one who died for us. Joseph remained loyal and committed to the God whom he believed and trusted even though the time of his release and opportunity for release did not come for two more years. Sometimes the proof of your commitment is not realized in the process that we are in but after we come through the struggle. Could you ever have known the focus and commitment in your life apart from the processes of God through trial and testing? Joseph certainly could not have known. He believed the vision and dreams he received and was very adamant to say what God showed to him. Yet he did not know the extent of the testing that would come to bring him into his purpose. God gives dreams and visions and prophetic promises which are generally stated as the completion of the process; ie, the end of the thing spoken or revealed. This then means He must take us to the beginning of the thing and walk us through it. How important is it to trust in His matchless wisdom. Who but God can do these kinds of things. You must remember that you are in process. When you are in process, not even other people can pull you out before the timing of God. Sometimes it will seem that you have been forgotten by people and that someone should how you ministered to them. How you cared for them and suffered to see them blessed. But, the Word of the Lord says in Romans 12:1;

"I beseech you therefore brethren, by the mercies of God, that ye present your bodies and living sacrifice, holy, acceptable unto God, which is your reasonable service."

We are not in this relationship with the creator of all things for us; but for him. Ecc. 12:13

"Let us hear the conclusion of the whole matter: Fear God, and keep his commandments; for this is the whole duty of man." We must allow the process of God to be completely accomplished in us because He will judge our works. **Verse 14**

"For God will bring every work into judgment, with every secret thing, whether it be good, or whether it be evil."

When we understand that every work will be judged; we note that it is to our best interests to allow God to lay in us the proper foundations so that we are equipped to be successful and produce fruit worthy of our repentance. John the Baptist told the leadership of his day; "Bring forth fruit that was meet for repentance." Matt. 3:8 He spoke these things knowing that he was dealing with a very traditional and heart hardened people. He called the Pharisees and Sadducees a generation of vipers. When we realize that God is bringing us into a process of change and we rebel against that change, we will, as did the Pharisees and Sadducees, become hard of heart and worthy of the title *GENERATION OF VIPERS*. Joseph did not resist God but submitted to the Word of Promise which was given to him. After two years then, Joseph is remembered by the Chief Butler in the house of Pharoah the King. Pharoah has had dreams and none in his kingdom can interpret the dreams. The Chief Butler then remembers Joseph as the one who had interpreted his dream and the dream of the Chief Baker. The Chief Butler tells the King of the gifting of Joseph and his ability to understand dream. Joseph is sent for by the Pharoah. God's desire after we have been proved is to send for us that we may administrate the affairs of Christ. This is an opportunity for the glory of the Lord to be revealed in Joseph on a national and international scale. Can God send for His sons and daughters to place them in the forefront of the world's condition and reveal His glory through us. Can the leaders of this world send for the men and women of God and trust the wisdom of God in them? Now we see that before Joseph can come into the presence of the Pharoah, he must shave and change his raiment. It then is up to us to begin to be prepared and equipped to stand in the places of authority and possess the land which has been given to us. Joseph has been prepared in the dungeon to meet the King. It is out of our seasons of brokenness that we are prepared to minister in the kings palace. The Apostle Paul was first imprisoned for his witness concerning the Lord Jesus Christ and then was sent to Rome to witness in the Kings palace. *And the night following the Lord stood by him, and said,* Rom. 23:11;

"Be of good cheer, Paul: for as thou hast testified of me in Jerusalem, so must thou bear witness also at Rome."

Also, Joseph is not the same brash young boy that he was when he received the dreams from God and shared them with his father and brothers. He is meek and humble in the prison and ready now to meet the King of Egypt. He has put on the raiment of humility as he prepares to go before the Pharoah. The people of God will be a violent generation in the Spirit. Yet in the natural they will be a humble and totally submitted and obedient people representing Jesus Christ in the earth.

It is curious that Pharoah is ready to receive Joseph based on the word of another individual. *(The Chief Butler)* Still we must know that men are searching for the truth. Many will hear us as they are entreated through the witness of others whom we have ministered to. Joseph ministered to the Chief Butler and God having set a season of preparation; has now brought Pharoah to the time of receiving Joseph. Pharoah is in need of someone to interpret the dreams he has had. In the interpreting the dreams, Joseph makes it clear to Pharoah that it is not in him that the interpretation originates but in God. The gifting comes from God. All of what we must do in the earth as the sons of the Living God, will ultimately be done as we walk in relationship with the Holy Spirit by faith. The walk of the believer is fully predicated on the relationship that we maintain regardless of circumstance. Often the struggle is compounded by the lack or failure to continue in Christ even though we have hardship. To sit down from responsibility, is to walk contrary to the will of God. God has given what he has given to increase fellowship with himself. It is not given so that we can dismiss it (the responsibility) because of circumstance. Your ministry is your walk of destiny. Everything which must be dealt with must be seen as a part of your growth in relationship with him.

Now, when we speak of these things, we are not talking about that which is given for diversion. There are those things, which are placed upon us, as a means of weighing us down. They are placed there so that we cannot do effectively that which is our purpose. Joseph knew very little of his purpose! Yet, all of the other problems and conditions had to be ministered through until that which was the real purpose for his being in Egypt was come. You must minister through the ordeal. Stay focused with what the Lord has placed in your life regarding your purpose. Again, when given the task of the speaking the things of God; there must be a discipline in the people of God to say only what He is saying. Joseph points out to Pharoah that the dream is given twice because it is established by God and that God would shortly bring it to pass. Gen. 41:32 People of the Lord; know what is established by God. Oftentimes, we are uncertain of what we speak. Because of difficulty trusting the Holy Spirit and having the assurance that what He has said is so; many move away from the responsibility of saying what God is saying. We abort the process in speaking the Word because we feel or believe that we are somehow responsible for bringing it to pass. This coupled with the holding of men?s persons in greater esteem than the ONE who called us becomes a stumbling block as well. Joseph's instruction for Pharoah concerning the dreams is such that Pharoah now favors Joseph. He does not favor Joseph because Joseph has elevated himself before the King. He favors Joseph because God has given Joseph wisdom and it is the wisdom needed for the market place. The Church must not be afraid of the market place. God is releasing an anointing for the market place into the Body of Christ and the people of God should realize that there is coming a transferring of wealth. This is born out in Proverbs 13:22b;

"the wealth of the sinner is laid up for the just."

It will sustain not only the nation of Egypt but nations which would come for help.

So then, Joseph?s first instruction to Pharoah is that He seek out a man discreet and wise to set over the land of Egypt. Vs.33 He further instructs that Pharoah appoint officers and take up the fifth part of the land. The Church needs to have the wisdom and revelation of God available as the world will be looking for insight and instruction to meet the impending crisis of circumstance and struggle. This can only happen through the preparation of the Holy Spirit in taking the people of God through the crisis of circumstances which have been resolved through testing. *STAY IN THE TEST!* You are being prepared to give an answer of the reason of hope that is within you with meekness and fear. Ist Peter 3:15 says;

"But sanctify the Lord God in your hearts: and be ready always to give an answer to every man that asketh you a reason of the hope that is in you with meekness and fear."

A part of the process of struggle is that of allowing God to be sanctified in your heart. God must bring the people of God to a place of separation for his purpose. The Lord desires to be first in us and He must have pre- eminence. John the Baptist said of Jesus in the inception of his ministry; ?He must increase but I must decrease. Beloved, God is calling for your demise. Not that you die literally, but that you mortify the deeds of your flesh that He may live in you.

Joseph has now come to the place in his relationship with the Father that he can be trusted to rule for the Fathers sake.

"And Pharoah said unto Joseph; forasmuch as God hath showed thee all this; there is none so discreet and wise as thou art."

God has now raised up Joseph to be great in Egypt over everyone except Pharoah. The strength of what has happened with Joseph can be recognized in this scripture when regarded by Pharoah as discreet and wise. Remember now that Joseph in initially having received the dreams which God gave him; was quick to reveal what had been shown him. This caused his brothers to hate him. But, now Joseph has come to a place of maturity in having learned the way of discretion with wisdom. To be discreet is described by Websters Dictionary as: *Having or showing a judicious reserve in one's speech or behavior respectful or propriety. It also means to lack ostentation or pretension, unobtrusive; modest.* **Perhaps the initial struggle for Joseph was one of wanting to show off in some way by bragging or boasting concerning the things he had seen and Gods plan to elevate him above his brethren. Joseph has been matured through the struggles that engaged his life and is now prepared for leadership. The people of God must see and know that their promotion comes from God. We must then, not allow the purpose in our lives to become a springboard for the will of the flesh. It is our purpose which gives us our reason**

for living. **Without understanding purpose many will live in futility and confusion. In the Hebrew the definition for discreet is bene: It means** *to separate mentally, understand, attend, consider, diligently, direct, discern and to have a prudent regard.* **Joseph in allowing the purpose of God to be worked in his life has come to a place where he now possesses a prudent regard for the will of the Living God. It takes a mental separation and discernment with focus to stay on track with ones purpose and not lose our perspective in the struggle. The greek translation for this word is that of** *reigning or curbing the midrift as a partition of the body.* **The people of The Lord cannot operate in their own thinking but must allow the Spirit of God to hold tight their reins. There is a discipline that the Body of Christ must come into. It is the discipline of being moved and directed by the Holy Spirit; not only by leading but** *by constraint.* (to compel by physical, moral, or circumstantial force) **The Church does not belong to itself. It belongs to the Lord. When we understand this and submit to His person we will begin to allow ourselves to put on His righteousness. This is referred to by The Apostle Paul in Ephesians 6:14 when he says;**

Stand, therefore, having your loins girt about with truth, having on the breastplate of righteousness."

Now Joseph has come to recognize the truth about himself in light of God?s Will for his life and has come completely obedient to God. Joseph is further referred to as wise and the lack of wisdom is the stronghold for failure in many lives. To be wise by definition means: *wise in mind, word, and act. It is the Hebrew word Chakam and further relates to making and showing wisdom.* **Many Christians are living for the stuff that the world has to offer. When they have received those things (stuff), they yet have no enjoyment or peace in them. But when we do the will of the Lord; we are encouraged and strengthened, while walking in peace and prosperity. God's focus for us is that of perpetual increase and blessing and He will not allow us to miss our blessing when we have been obedient to the will of His Spirit. The times when we feel alone and forgotten are many times the place where the Holy Spirit is attempting to do a work in us. Your separation for a time or season is not necessarily a bad thing. Joseph is apparently forgotten and that in**

light of the positive ministry he has done in the name of the Lord. Still, he continues to serve and finally is revealed by God to Pharoah. God will reveal you in your season and your gift will make room for you. This elevation as second only to Pharoah, brings a fulfilling of the dreams of Joseph but are not all that God has prepared for Joseph.

CHAPTER SIX

"THE PROMOTION"
Genesis 41:40

"Thou shalt be over my house, and according unto thy word shall all my people be ruled: only in the throne will I be greater than thou."

God is desirous to give the Church absolute rule in the earth. We know that at the time of the ascension of Jesus; there was a delegating of authority to the Body of Christ. In Matthew 28:18, Jesus said;

"all power is given unto me in heaven and in earth."

This power is given to the people of the Lord for a demonstration of the authority of Christ and His Bride (The Church) in the earth against the kingdom of the devil. Yet, the Church has remained virtually powerless because it has failed to endure the trials of struggle that have been a part of its calling and mandate. There have been pockets of yielding and submission in the Body of Christ, but the level and focus of elevation which God desires have been unapproached. Without this level of submission and obedience with dedication and commitment; *(teaching them to observe all things whatsoever I have commanded:)* **vs. 20;** The Church is destined to fail. It cannot continue to operate in the will of men and hope to do that which is beyond the ability of men to perform. The sons of Jacob believed that Joseph was missing the mark because his vision went beyond what they could see in the natural. Many in the Church world have difficulty believing and accepting the move of the Spirit of God in this hour. It is because you cannot access the things of Christ except by the Spirit. God will not operate according to men's flesh. *Joseph is elevated by the Spirit of God because he has been taught to walk by the Spirit of God.* The processing through which Joseph is come has prepared him for the elevation. Pharoah has done what was already prepared in the Spirit Realm by God for Joseph. Joseph because of his humbleness and submission to God's purpose has now come to the time of his promotion and is able to not only receive it, but is able to be trusted with the responsibility given to him; first by God and then by Pharoah. Pharoah then places his ring upon Joseph's hand as a show of the transfer of power and authority within the kingdom. Not only is a ring given but he is arrayed in vesture of fine linen and a gold chain placed about his neck. Whereas the coat of many colors has been taken from Joseph and his place in the heart of his father is lost for a time; Joseph is now given vestures of fine linen which is an allusion to the personal righteousness of Joseph. They are the garments of priestly anointing and symbolic of the righteousness of Christ. In Revelation 19:7- 8;

"Let us be glad and rejoice and give honor to Him; for the marriage of the lamb is come and his wife has made herself ready. And to her was granted that she should be arrayed in fine linen clean and white for the fine linen is the righteousness of the saints."

The preparation in struggle is that of making The Church ready to wear *the garments of righteousness* which are a symbol of the personal change that has taken place in the hearts of men. The gold chain around Joseph's neck points to his elevation into the kingly anointing and authority. It also represents the divine nature of God as revealed in the lives of men. God has given witness in the promotion of Joseph by Pharoah, that this is his righteous son. The glory of the Lord now rests upon Joseph. The next step in the elevation of Joseph is that of being given by Pharoah, the kings second chariot and the command that every subject of the kingdom should bow before Joseph. Joseph has now seen the elevation of God; as testified to by the Pharoah himself, in making him to ride in the king's chariot. God will give to The Church the authority of God as it comes into total obedience to the purposes of Christ. It is the kind of witness which is revealed in the signs and wonders which follow the speaking of the truth and heart of God. Hebrews chapter 2:3- 4 tell us;

"How shall we escape, if we neglect so great salvation, which at the first began to be spoken by the Lord, and was confirmed unto us by them that heard him; vs. 4; God also bearing them witness, with both signs and wonders, and with divers miracles and gifts of the Holy Ghost according to his own will"?

There then is a need for the Body of Christ to become completely obedient to the purposes of Christ and to stand in the Holy Place. This means that there is a place of intimacy with God that invokes the miraculous presence and power of God. It is intimated by the action of faith and obedience that exceeds the will and desires of men. Much of the struggle to be endured by the Church is born out of the carnality of living in the will of the flesh and not in the Spirit. This then will not allow the people of the Lord to approach the Throne of Grace in its own wisdom and strength. We must come by faith in Christ's redemptive work and the shed blood of Jesus. This should compel us to walk in the spirit of confession and repentance continually. Not as a legalistic display of a hypocritical ambivalence and disdain but of genuine resolve to obey the one who died for our sins. It is further not just to fellowship with Him but also the fellowship of the saints of God together with Him. Titus 3:3 shows us that;

"For we ourselves also were sometimes foolish, disobedient, deceived, serving divers lusts and pleasures, living in malice and envy, hateful and hating one another. But after that the kindness and love of God our savior toward man appeared, not by works of righteousness which we have done, but according to his mercy he saved us by the washing of regeneration, and renewing of the Holy Ghost."

When the prophetic word of the Lord is released over the life of an individual; it is the job of God's Holy Spirit to bring the fulfillment of that word. The only hindrance to the completion of that word in the life of the believer is the agreement of their will with what God said. This is true because God has made everyman his own moral agent. Joseph's agreement with the will of God had been activated in his will. You cannot accomplish the purpose for which you were intended unless you agree with the one who called you to purpose. Several changes have now occurred in the life of Joseph as a result of allowing the process of trial to be proved in his life. The first is that of Joseph being given a new name by Pharoah. It is a name that describes the call of Joseph in the eyes of the King. Joseph is called Zaphnath- paaneah which in Coptic means: *"The man to whom secrets are revealed."* Pharoah recognizes the prophetic gift that is in Joseph and gives him a name appropriate to the gifting. He is not intimidated by the mandate of God which is on the life of Joseph. *Note here that the change of name denotes a change in relationship.* Joseph has now gone from the prison to the kings palace and is no longer a slave in Egypt but a ruler. Joseph has endured the suffering and embarrassment of being sold into slavery and all the difficulty which ensued; but now his blessing is before him and God proves him in the king's palace. God would like to prove the people of the Lord in the earth and establish them before the world with the glory of the Lord resting upon us. The world at times is wiser than the Church or Body of Christ. It will use the call and gifting that is in an individual's life and will not be embarrassed or ashamed of its benefit. Yet the Church will denigrate or dismiss its own as though they were both ashamed and embarrassed to see or know the presence of God in them. We must allow the gifts and callings of God to come forth in the body and embrace them as the presence and power of God to perform His will in the Body of Christ. Ephesians 4:13 tells us that these gifts were given;

"till we all come into the unity of the faith, and of the knowledge of the Son of God, unto the measure of the stature of the fullness of Christ."

Until Christ is perfected in the people of the Lord; these gifts must operate and they must operate in the whole of the body. Ephesians 4:16 says;

"From whom the whole body fitly joined together and compacted by that which every joint supplieth, according to the effectual working in the measure of every part, maketh increase of the body unto the edifying of itself in love."

Joseph's brothers forgot that love was the key ingredient to their relationship with their brother Joseph. They hated him so much that it also affected the love they held for their father Jacob. They wounded deeply their father in order to be rid of Joseph who was their father's favorite son. The Body of Christ must not forget this example and do the love. Our hatred of one person will affect the love that we have for others. The second change which take place in the life of Joseph is that Pharoah not only changes the name of Joseph but also gives him a wife named Asenath which means: *one who is a goddess of the Egyptians.* While she is a pagan worshipper; this action shows the value and respect that the Pharoah holds for Joseph and the favor of the Lord that is given into his life. Joseph is given the very best that the king has to offer for the wisdom and gifting that is in his life. It is however, Joseph's righteousness to follow after the heart of God that gives him favor with both God and man. God wants to promote the Body of Christ in the earth. He desires to establish the wisdom and power of God in the world through The Church. The Church however, must first get God's heart. *Endure the trial!!!* Ist Peter chapter 1:5- 7 states;

''who are kept by the power of God through faith unto salvation ready to be revealed in the last time. Wherein ye greatly rejoice, though for a season, if need be, ye are in heaviness through manifold temptations; that the trial of your faith being much more precious than gold that perisheth, though it be tried with fire, might be found unto praise and honor and glory at the appearing of Jesus Christ.''

It is dangerous to give power and authority to them that do not possess the thoughts and desires and vision of Christ as their motivation and reason for living. *No hidden agenda can be enforced as the will of Christ.* Much of what hinders the Church is captured in the carnal and fleshly mind and will of men who desire to operate independently of Christ's purpose. It is a subtle kind of rebellion that lingers to keep the heart of God from coming forth. Yet, men say I have the mind of Christ but have not his HEART OR SPIRIT. You can only get the heart and spirit of Christ by spending time with him. Your trial should compel you to spend time with Him. Thirdly with this marriage comes also two sons; one named Manasseh: *which means; that God has made him to forget all his labor or toil, and his father house.* Joseph has come to the place in his relationship with God that he blesses everything that God does in his life and forgets those things which are past. Much of the struggle in the people of the Lord is continual in their inability to lay down the cares of the past. But, the Apostle Paul said;

Brethren, I count not myself to have apprehended; but this one thing I do, forgetting those things which are behind and reaching forth unto those things which are before, I press toward the mark for the prize of the high calling of God in Christ Jesus."

We as the servants of the Lord must understand that we cannot dwell in the failures and brokenness of the past. We must press into the fullness of our purpose and calling in God. Joseph has overcome the sense of loss and hurt which he felt after his betrayal at the hands of his brothers. Joseph's second son is called Ephraim in Genesis 41:52;

For God hath caused me to be fruitful in the land of my affliction."

Much of the time, the Christian has a very narrow focus in the midst of their struggle because they have not understood the ability of the Living God to perform great blessing in the middle of the struggle. Joseph named his son fruitful because he realized that the Lord had blessed him and made him fruitful in the adverse circumstances of his life. Joseph is afflicted and yet abounds in producing fruit. The birth of this son is an outward witness of what has transpired in Joseph despite the struggle. James chapter 5:13a speaks concerning the issue of personal affliction in this manner;

"Is any among you afflicted? Let him pray."

This word affliction means: *to inflict physical or mental suffering upon; cause grievous distress to; trouble seriously.* Joseph has had affliction and endured in the process through prayer and God has blessed him to be fruitful despite the conditions that were personal to him in struggle. The people of the Lord must begin to *embrace the affliction* as an opportunity to seek the face of the Lord and to know his perfect will even though hardship and sometimes very great loss is come. The anguish that we sometimes feel in the hurt and brokenness does not negate the faithfulness of a wise and caring God who is bringing us to purpose. Because God is faithful we cannot fail in our situation and trial unless we give up. The Word of God records Proverbs 24:10;

"if we faint in the time of adversity our strength is small."

Do not miss your opportunity to be fruitful. Jesus in John the 15th chapter speaks concerning the need to remain in the vine and produce fruit. If **we leave the vine we can do nothing. The Church must abide in Him, and He in The Church. While generally this statement is in individual terms of relationship; it is also the strength of what The Church is to become as a collective body. Now, with the promotion of Joseph and his new station in Egypt; there is that wisdom and authority which must come forth to preserve the nation in the time of its crisis. This is the season for which Joseph has been prepared and with God's help he will do all that is glorious and powerful in the mind and heart of God. Oftentimes; the challenge for God's people is one of trusting the wisdom that He has placed in them for ministry. There is a struggle that comes to undermine the confidence that the people of the Lord need to use in walking out the will of Christ successfully. Even though we have been delivered from the affliction and have gained wisdom and knowledge of what to do and how to do; we still must remain completely dependent upon Him. This is an issue of trust. Joseph does not move away from the relationship that has developed as a result of his testing. Joseph now has come to the time of seven bountiful years of harvest, and the wisdom that was revealed in the interpretation the King's dreams is put into place. He prepares all of Egypt to face the famine that is to come. We must begin to employ the wisdom of God that has been given to us as a result of the struggle that the Lord has brought us through. Stay in the trial until the Lord reveal the wisdom. Often there is an aborting of the process which is intended for your equipping and the wisdom is lost. The net result of the employment of this wisdom is that of not only being prepared for the famine, but of being able to live through the famine. The famine was over all the earth and Egypt was the place that God chose to sustain life in the earth.**

"And all countries came into Egypt to Joseph for to buy corn; because that the famine was so sore in all lands."

CHAPTER SEVEN

SIMEON: "THE HOSTAGE"
Genesis 42:1- 2

"Now when Jacob saw that there was corn in Egypt, Jacob said to his sons, why do ye look one upon another? And he said, behold I have heard that there is corn in Egypt: get you down thence; that we may live, and not die."

There has come the time now when Jacob has compelled his sons to go to Egypt to buy grain. Oftentimes in the body of Christ, there is a vascillating which takes place. It is the times of our uncertainty and insecurity in seeing what needs to be done and taking the initiative to do those things. Much of the struggle of believers is that of knowing what to do and then not doing it. James 4:17 declares;

"Therefore, to him that knoweth to do good and doeth it not, to him it is sin."

There are many confrontations that take place in the walking out of the Will of The Lord in our lives and much of the need to be obedient is captured in our willingness to do the thing we know is right according to the Word of God. Yet they must be told by their father to go and buy food so that they can live. How often is it, that the struggle to walk in submission to all that God has commanded is born out of the compelling of others to obey. If we do not get and maintain a relationship with the Father for ourselves; then our total liberty or obedience is predicated on someone else's direction or leading. The NEED to live is a key ingredient to our survival in the earth. Yet Jesus says in John?s Gospel the 10th chapter and the 10th verse;

"The thief cometh not, but for to steal, and to kill, and to destroy: I am come that they might have life and that they might have it more abundantly."

There can be no abundance apart from the giver and sustainer of life. There must be in the body of Christ a whole-hearted commitment and drive to LIVE, which will cause us to endure every challenge to that need in our lives. The Church must LIVE!!!

A further evidence of the need to live and to maintain life is experienced in the reluctance of Jacob to send his youngest son Benjamin with his ten brethren. Jacob does not trust his sons with the life of Benjamin because they failed to return home to him Joseph. Jacob has mourned the absence of Joseph and is not willing to allow anything to befall him. Genesis 42:4b The people of the Lord have a responsibility to protect the innocent of the Father. There is the need to see the generations of the Lord after us come into their destinies. It is the mandate of the scripture that *the Fathers lay up an inheritance for the Children.* Proverbs 13:22a says;

"A good man leaveth an inheritance to his children's children."

There should then be the expectation that our children will be preserved to come into their inheritance. Jacob was not willing to see Benjamin cut off from him.

Now with this has come the fulfillment of the prophecies and dreams which Joseph has had. It is this very issue which has seen Joseph sold into slavery and thrown into prison. Consummately, it has led to the promotion of Joseph in the house of Pharoah and the kingdom of Egypt. At there coming into Egypt the brothers of Joseph are in fact compelled by custom to display their humility by bowing in the presence of kings and royalty. This is their initial display of compliance with the Prophetic Word. The fact that men disagree with the Prophetic Word does not mean that that word is a false word. It must be understood that the Word of the Lord is greater than men's opinion. Joseph's brothers have come to the land; and having bowed before Joseph they do not recognize him. It is curious that many in your inception as the man or woman of God will not be able to recognize you. God has spoken His Word over your life but your life does not as yet measure up to what he said. We may have the calling of God in our lives but the grace of the office and anointing must be worked out by relationship with Him. Joseph had the calling and saw by dreams and vision what would be the results of his obedience to God. But, he had not walked those things out until this time had come. When you see or hear His Word; get set to walk it out. Joseph's brothers did not realize that what Joseph had spoken to them was yet to be walked out in the life of Joseph: that time would be the indicator of whether those things were true. Through this they lost relationship with Joseph and severely wounded their father Jacob with their deceptions.

After coming to Egypt they are challenged by Joseph to prove that they are not spies. Joseph tries his brothers and placed them in ward for 3 days. Perhaps there is a measure of desire in Joseph to hold them accountable for the way they have treated him in the past. Although we find out that, Joseph comes to them after the 3rd day and releases them all except Simeon. Simeon epresents the worst in his brothers for cruelty and viciousness. He is forced to become surety in the place of his brothers as they return home to care for their fathe and their families. This also is a type of intercession that represents the sacrifice made without choice. Remember that Simeon and Levi were the brothers who plotted and schemed to kill the men of Shechem because Shechem raped their sister Dinah. Gen. 34:2 *"And when Shechem the son of Hamor the Hivite, prince of the country, saw her, he took her, and lay with her, and defiled her."*

Oftentimes; there are those things in our lives that will show the severity of the life we have lived and this is evident with Levi and Simeon. They agreed with the men of Shechem, that if they would be circumcised as they were; they would agree to a marriage between Dinah and Shechem the son of Hamor. Simeon and Levi waited 3 days before they assaulted the city and killed all the males of the city and then the sons of Jacob took the spoil. Simeon and Levi were not merciful men in their wrath. This is a *breach in the spirit* because they have murdered innocent people who were not involved in the sin of Shechem and it is born out in the word spoken over their lives by Jacob in blessing his sons before he dies. *Genesis 49:5- 7 tells us;*

"Simeon and Levi are brethren; instruments of cruelty are in their habitations. O my soul, come not thou into their secret; unto their assembly, mine honor be not thou united: for in their anger they slew a man, and in their selfwill they have digged down a wall. Cursed be their anger, for it was fierce, and their wrath, for it was cruel: I will divide them in Jacob, and scatter them in Israel."

Joseph however is not the vindictive and bitter person that develops because he is focused on revenge or getting even for what has been done against him. He has matured in the trial and struggles of his life and is now set to heal and restore his brethren rather than destroy them.

Lets note here that there have been many wounded relationships in the Body of Christ which have resulted because of the *lack of understanding.* There are many broken relationships that are not healed because of a lack the discipline in trial and testing to bring us to a place of maturity. Maturity is recognizing that God's heart is that, of reconciliation and restoration. The need for trust is sorely tested in The Church.

Now all relationship is only as good or purposeful as the ability of the parties involved to trust. The Church doesn't know its? members. How can we trust one whom we have not spent time with. Our level of commitment is based on the time spent. Joseph is willing to reconcile because he has spent time not just being incarcerated, but by searching The Spirit of God. *Again he has a relationship.* Consequently Simeon is the one that Joseph keeps, not because Joseph is angry or bitter with him or his brothers, but because he desires to be reconciled. This is apparent in his willingness in the 3rd day to allow them to return home to feed their families. He gives them the stipulation that they are not to return unless they bring Benjamin. Joseph is making sure to hold them in a place of necessity, so that they can't move away from him and he lose the ability to see his brother Benjamin. Genesis 42:20

"But bring your youngest brother unto me; so shall your words be verified and ye shall not die. And they did so."

Hear now; there is constraint in The Spirit Realm for the people of the Lord to be reconciled. 0Because of this, the people of the Lord that know God's heart for healing and to reconcile The Body of Christ; must be diligent to do everything within its power to affect that purpose in the earth. Joseph is prepared to make a difference! We are expected to make a difference in all that we do *because our spirit has influence* and this cannot be taken lightly. Therefore, we cannot dismiss the importance of being obedient to the will of God. Paul told the Corinthians in Ist Corinthians 6:17;

"but he that is joined unto the Lord is one spirit."

In the book of Romans in the 6 chapter th he told the Roman Church*; '*

"know ye not, that to whom ye yield yourselves servants to obey, his servants ye are to whom ye obey; whether of sin unto death, or of obedience unto righteousness"?

In this process of restoration there is submission that must come. Joseph, through the time he has spent, isolated from his brethren; has been prepared by God for kingship and priestly authority. He is brought through this process to fulfill the purpose for which he is intended. He must suffer to learn how to obey God. Hebrews 5:8 says of Christ;

"Though he were a son, yet learned he obedience by the things which he suffered."

As much as his brethren have sinned against Joseph; *they yet remain the children of God* and that first and foremost is in the understanding of Joseph. Joseph knew that he had gone through these things to prepare the way for those that would follow. Oftentimes; we may not understand all the particulars of the circumstances we find ourselves in; yet we must realize that the God of creation has a plan for us. It is in the suffering and enduring of the process that we are learning to obey Him. It is in the process that we are made Godly. Thanks be to God for his infinite wisdom and grace.

At this point we must take notice of the guilt and condemnation that is yet stirring in the hearts and minds of the Joseph's brothers. It has been as much now as 17 years since Joseph has seen his brothers and they yet have not resolved their issues of guilt. Genesis 42:22

"And Rueben answered them, saying, Spake I not unto you, saying, do not sin against the child; and ye would not hear; therefore behold, also his blood is required."

All relationship involves blood as a part of it's covenant. God expects the people of the Lord to hold covenant as an integral part of their relationship and experience together. Therefore we cannot allow relationship that has been broken to remain broken. It is a matter of covenant and blood is always required in covenant. The Spirit of reconciliation is God?s heart for the Body of Christ and a continual urging of his people to be ye reconciled is his theme. Romans 5:10

"For if when we were enemies, we were reconciled to God by the death of his Son, much more being reconciled we shall be saved by his life."

If Christ then has done these things for us; how can The People of The Lord do less?

The brothers because of the conviction of the Lord cannot forget that they have sinned against their brother and are constantly reminded that they have deceived their father Jacob. This too is a testing of the brothers, to come into obedience and reconciliation as well. Please know and understand that where God has been preparing you for reconciliation and restoration: He as well is working to prepare others for that season of coming into obedience. Because of this there are long struggles that follow our failure in relationships. They have followed because we have not understood that our concern should be the same as the Fathers. His concern is that of esteeming others and to embrace them; even in their differences. Because Joseph was different, he became an outcast. Division and separation are not the heart of the Father. His desire is that of celebrating the differences in his people. Again our differences show the diversity of the Creator in giving and sustaining all life. *Our differences should not make a difference or cause division.*

Here then is the time to assess the things that have happened with the coming of the brothers of Joseph into the land of Egypt. Joseph's brothers are now before him and have not recognized him as their brother. They could not see the promise of God in him. Additionally there is a need for Joseph to find a way to reconcile with them. He decides to keep them in ward for 3 days and then to keep Simeon while the others go and attend their families. Further he decides that they should not come back to see him unless they bring their youngest brother. Again there is a need in Joseph to insure that he not only can see his brother Benjamin but also his father Jacob. With this then he sent the other nine brothers back to his father and has restored their monies to their sacks. Joseph does not desire to benefit himself or the Pharoah in anyway at the expense of his family. To that end he is gracious and shows great compassion upon them. They however, are suspicious when they find the monies restored to them and have no explanation for their father as to why it was restored. The simple truth is that Joseph loved his brothers and his father and desired to bless them. The heart of the living God is for his people to love one another unconditionally. Love desires to benefit someone else at the expense of itself, with no desire for anything in return. *Joseph simply loved them!*

CHAPTER EIGHT

"PREPARATION FOR BENJAMIN"
Genesis 42:35; 43:1- 34

This is the time now, when the sons of Jacob have returned to him with grain to sustain them. They begin to explain everything that has happened in Egypt to their father. Jacob has seen the provision that has come to him from Egypt but is made afraid over the monies which has been restored to the sacks of his sons. This is not the least of the concern that Jacob has regarding those things; which he has heard from his sons. They have informed him that they cannot return to Egypt without Benjamin as evidence that they are not spies. This along with the monies that has been found in their sacks is distressing to Jacob.

And it came to pass as they emptied their sacks that behold, every man?s bundle of money was in his sack; and when both they and their father saw the bundles of money, they were afraid. And Jacob their father said unto them, Me have ye bereaved of my children, Joseph is not and Simeon is not, and ye will take Benjamin away: all these things are agains me."

Genesis 42:35- 36 Rueben, who is the eldest son and the one to whom the birthright should fall stands forward and speaks his willingness to be surety for Benjamin. In verse 37;

"and Rueben spake unto his father, saying, slay my two sons, if I bring him not to thee; deliver him into my hand, and I will bring him to thee again. Vs. 38; and he said, my son shall not go down with you; for his brother is dead and he is left alone.

If mischief befall him by the way in the which ye go, then shall ye bring down my gray hairs with sorrow to the grave."

Whereas Rueben has had the responsibility before for his brother Joseph, and Joseph was lost; Jacob refuses to allow Benjamin to go with Rueben. Jacob does not trust Rueben with this responsibility. Jacob had issues of trust and could not bring himself to allow his youngest son to go to Egypt. He believed that it was too great a risk particularly with that responsibility entrusted to Reuben. What we cannot risk is the very thing that we value most. However, there is a place of submission and obedience that God desires to bring every believer into. It is an assurance that no condition is greater than His ability to keep us.

NOTE: Often, we do certain things because there isn?t any other choice; save the extremity of loss. So now; it is the loss of a whole family as opposed to the potential loss of Benjamin his youngest son that Jacob must make. Genesis 43:1 *"And the famine was sore in the land."*

It's at this point, because of the famine in the land; that Jacob must send his sons back to Egypt for more grain. He is charged by Judah, concerning the words spoken to them by Joseph. In Genesis 43:3- 5;

"And Judah spake unto him, saying, the man did solemnly protest unto us, saying, ye shall not see my face except your brother be with you. Vs. 4; if thou wilt send our brother with us, we will go down and buy thee food; Vs. 5; but if thou wilt not send him, we will not go down; for the man said unto us, ye shall not see my face except your brother be with you."

There has now come the time where Jacob's sons become more assertive in their regard for what has been spoken to them by Joseph. They have become determined not to return without Benjamin. Reuben has not only lost the respect of his father because of his failure to protect Joseph; but he has violated the sanctity of his father's couch. That is, he has sought to possess the birthright of his father by having his Father's concubine. Gen 49:3- 4; gives us clarity about this.

"Reuben thou art my firstborn, my might, and the beginning of my strength. The excellency of dignity and the excellency of power. Vs. 4; Unstable as water, thou shalt not excel; because thou wentest up to the Father's bed an defilest it: he went up to my couch."

NOTE: Much of what has faced The Church is born out of the folly of The Church. There have been many conditions of hypocrisy and tradition in The Body of Christ. Men have showed Jesus Christ as some kind of godless, immoral, mystic; that could not possibly do and accomplish what he said. They have made him a God without power or righteousness. Consequently, the world is not impressed with our God. Rueben could not be trusted with the responsibility of HEADSHIP. The giving or passing of the birthright is always about headship. It is apostolic principal for setting in order and giving structure to the purposes of God in the earth. Headship ministry has the responsibility of setting order and structure in the family.

Jacob then, is confronted with the uncertainty of his condition. The ones he loved the most are in jeopardy of being lost to him. He must decide for the sake of all of his children. Judah then assures him in verse 8;

"And Judah said unto Israel his father, send the lad with me, and we will arise and go, that we may live, and not die, both we, and thou, and also our little ones. Vs. 9; I will be surety for him; of my hand shalt thou require him: if I bring him not unto thee and set him before thee then let me bear the blame forever."

Now, even though Jacob is reluctant to send Benjamin his son to Egypt; he is willing to trust Judah with his security and safety. I would like to say at this point that The Church is very much responsible for the will of God being demonstrated in the earth. It is the call of the Father in us to be responsible for the safety and well being of the lost. It is not that we can save anyone but it is the idea of The Church accepting the responsibility to become surety for the lost. That surety then becomes intercessory as the body of Christ begins to pray out that responsibility as a covering and gapstanding entity in the Spirit Realm. The net result is the Harvest that is garnered. Jesus told his disciples to look out on the fields because they were ripe for harvest. In Luke 10:2;

"Therefore said he unto them, the harvest truly is great, but the labourers are few: pray ye therefore the Lord of the harvest, that he would send forth labourers into his harvest."

There is a *mandate in the Spirit* for what the Lord desires to do in bringing souls into the Kingdom of God. Notice now the prayer of Jacob as he sends Judah and the others away to Egypt:

"And God almighty give you mercy before the man, that he may send away your other brother, and Benjamin. If I be bereaved of my children, I am bereaved."

Let's go back then and look at a very pivotal set of statements that were made by Jacob and their significance to his sons return to Egypt. In verses 11 and 12 of Genesis 43, Jacob comments on what must take place in their return trip.

"And their father Israel said unto them, If it must be so now, do this; tak of the best fruits in the land in your vessels, and carry down the man a present, a little balm, and a little honey, spices, and myrrh, nuts, and almonds: And take double money in your hand; and the money that was brought again in the mouth of your sacks, carry it again in your hand; peradventure it was an oversight."

There is now the need to bring an offering to Joseph. This is a type and shadow of The Church and its need to render sacrifice to the God of our salvation. Often, the People of the Lord, desire to come into His presence without bringing a *holy offering.* God in the book of Genesis chapter 4 distinguishes between the offering of Cain and his brother Abel. He notes that Cain's offering is unacceptable while the offering of Abel is accepted. *Verses 3- 5*

"And in the process of time it came to past, that Cain brought of the fruit of the ground an offering unto the Lord. And Abel, he also brought of the firstlings of his flock and of the fat thereof. And the Lord had respect unto Abel and to his offering: But unto Cain and to his offering he had not respect. And Cain was very wroth, and his countenance fell."

There is a liberty that God has given to us in His grace, to bring us into the presence of the Lord. *It is a way that he has set which cannot be abridged or circumvented through the will of the flesh. Men must love the works of God. They must do that which is commanded His way.* The Lord told Cain;

'If thou doest well, shalt thou not be accepted? And if thou doest not well, sin lieth at the door: and unto thee shall be his desire and thou shalt rule over him."

God commands that we enter into his gates with thanksgiving and into his courts with praise; that we are to be thankful unto him and bless his name. Often there is a complacency that permeates the churches and ambivalence for the presence of God. God is calling the people of the Lord, into TRUE WORSHIP. This is that place of submission to Christ where men begin to give up their will and desire. We then embrace the will and desire of the Christ who called us to relationship. It is a living expression of the character of Christ because we have accepted his word as the absolute rule for our living; and in living in his word we become a true expression of worship to him. Worship is about who Christ is. We then worship Him in relationship because of who he has become to us. Therefore, He has desired to bring his will to fullness in the lives of those who will obey the Word of God. True worship reflects the image of the person, place, or thing that is worshipped. With this then, we become a reflection of Christ in the earth. First we become a reflection in Him and then to Him and finally, for Him. This means that we are to search the Word of God to know his heart and will for our lives and as we know his heart we become transformed into his image and likeness. Rom. 8:29

"For whom he foreknew, He also predestined to be conformed to the image of His Son that He might be the firstborn among many brethren."

This is reflection in him. Then as we begin to reflect him and Christ begins to see himself in us; God then unveils us and makes that reflection to be seen in the earth by others. Rom. 8:19

'For the earnest expectation of the creature waiteth for the manifestation of the sons of God."

Please know beloved that becoming the likeness of Him requires being hidden from the purview of men and many times embroiled in much struggle and conflict. God will allow many trials and testing before he brings promotion. This is much of the difficulty of serving the Lord for many. The Church and Churchfolks want instant approval and recognition and anointings. Remember Reuben: Rueben lost the understanding that the promotion or birthright would belong to the one who held his Father's heart. These things take trial and conflict and observing to seek the face of the Father for his heart. In discovering the Father's heart, we see ourselves then challenged to change. If we are unwilling to change as we see Him; we are prevented from becoming His image and unable to fulfill our purpose. Oftentimes, it would seem that many of the giftings and abilities that we possess are hidden and the need to express ourselves in purpose is muted. It is not that God has a desire to keep us from our purpose but, that we not be lost to the fullness of His will by premature exposure. If Christ would allow us to go when we felt ready; many would be shipwrecked. However, God is preserving his investment and keeping us from the snares of the adversary.

CHAPTER NINE

"THE FATHERING SPIRIT"

Let us now consider that there has come a change into the earth because of the shifting in the Spirit realm. God is releasing revelation for the sake of establishing the end time authority of the Church in the earth. The first aspect of this revelation is found in Malachi 4:5- 6.

"Behold I will send you Elijah the Prophet before the coming of the great and terrible day of the Lord. Vs. 6 And he shall turn the heart of the fathers to the children and the heart of the children to their fathers, lest I come and smite the earth with a curse."

For far too long the Church has lived in obscurity, limited by its lack of knowledge and understanding. In Luke 1:17 we find John the Baptist giving representation to this as the forerunner of Christ.

"And he shall go before him in the spirit and power of Elias, to turn the hearts of the father to the children, and the disobedient to the wisdom of the just; to make ready a people prepared for the Lord."

So then we see the first evidence of a Fathering Spirit that is the birthing of the Apostolic office of God in the earth. Note as well, that God says that if this does not come *He would smite the earth with a curse.* It is this Spirit that makes the way for Christ to be born in the earth. In this; God in his wisdom has given the Five- fold ministry of Christ to his Body; that it may be equipped and released to fulfill it's mandate. He gave the anointing of

the Apostolic Office to set the order and the structure of God in the Church. 1st Cor. 12:28

"And God has set some in the Church, first apostles, secondarily prophets and thirdly teachers, after that miracles, then gifts of healing, helps, governments, diversities of tongues."

Much of the struggle and turmoil of the Body of Christ is a resistance to that alignment and agreement that is mandated. Joseph, in charging his brothers, gains the respect that was missing in his being sold initially. Had his brothers respected him first and foremost, Joseph would have not been placed in such struggle. Let us digress for a moment and address the issue of the Apostolic Office. Much of mainstream Christianity has been non-accepting of the truth regarding the Office of the Apostle. Because of this they have not been willing to transition into alignment with God's purpose. In addressing this issue it became necessary to question whether or not their statements are valid in dismissing this office. Many of the statements have to do with whether or not it was a work of God only in the time of Christ and the immediate work of the Holy Spirit after his ascension. Yet in seeking to understand this issue I ask the Lord why there was such difficulty in accepting the Word of God as absolute truth. His question to me was; Has anything changed in this dispensation? I answered no Sir. *He said to me then that nothing could change in what he had said unless the dispensation changed.* **If then we remove or change any part of this Word of God, we make ourselves liable for the curses of scripture. We must know that the Bible is a book of structure and order.** *It does not line up with us; we line up with it.* **The old prophetic order to has watered down and made of no effect the Word of God. Not as much by what has been done alone, but by a failure to receive the heart of Christ and minister in the wisdom of the Spirit of God. We must first believe that the Word of God is absolute truth. The Apostle Paul told Timothy to preach the Word. The mandate of the Apostles Office is one of preaching the revelation of God for this day that we live in and it is built foundationally on what has already been revealed in the Word of God. Apostolic order must operate in the Church to enable the Body of Christ to be perfected. The Church has operated in a 3- fold anointing but Paul told the Ephesians in chapter 4 and verse 11 that the operation of the**

ministry in the earth was 5- fold. In verse 12 he said that they were given for the perfecting of the saints. Our next question to be answered is; has the Church been perfected? This is somewhat a mute point, since obviously it has not. How then can these things become ordered when firstly; the chief anointing for structure and order rests with the Apostle. Not only will they operate in structure and order as Apostles, but secondarily; in the foundation and framing of the Body: Ephesians 2:20- 22;

"and are built upon the foundation of the Apostles and Prophets, Jesus Christ himself being the chief cornerstone; In whom all the building fitly framed together groweth unto a holy temple in the Lord: In whom ye are also builded together for an habitation of God through the Spirit."

But thirdly, as those that empower The Body of Christ: in Ephesians 3:3;

"How that by revelation he made known unto me the mystery; (as I wrote afore in few words, Whereby, when ye read, ye may understand my knowledge in the mystery of Christ); which in other ages was not made known unto the sons of men, as it is now revealed unto his holy apostles and prophets by the Spirit."

Further it is the initial mandate of the office in Ephesians 4:12;

"for the perfecting of the saints, for the work of the ministry, for the edifying of the body of Christ."

The Church cannot be empowered without the revelation of Christ or the ministry of the Apostle. Fourthly; the gift of administration must be released in the Church. *In I Cor.12:28 the authority is established for the Apostle as an administrator.*

"And God has set some in the church, firstly Apostles, secondarily Prophets, thirdly Teachers, after that miracles, then gifts of healings, helps, governments, diversities of tongues.?" II Cor.11:28; "besides those things which are without, that which cometh upon me daily, the care of all the churches."

In Acts 15, there is a question regarding the need in the Church to be circumcised after the manner of Moses. Because of the disputing that followed; Paul and Barnabas decided to go to Jerusalem to confer with the Apostles and elders. When the Apostles and Elders came together to consider this matter, they received testimony from Peter as well as Paul and Barnabas. In verse 13th it says that the Apostle James gave direction concerning what should be done of them in the matter. This instruction is given by apostolic mandate. Then the Word of God says that they sent men of their own to accompany Paul and Barnabas to Antioch. Vs 22 They also sent letters and greetings along with their instruction and wisdom. Vs 23 There is much in the way of Apostolic administration to help effect the Body of Christ in righteousness. Finally, there is the release of miracles to the body that must flow through the Apostolic Office. In this same chapter of Acts 15 in the 12th verse Paul and Barnabas th give evidence to miracles and wonders that God had wrought among the Gentiles by them. God is bringing a mighty flow of miracles into the Church and they will be released through the Apostolic Authority.

That is why in the initial dreams of Joseph we find a continuing difficulty with order and alignment between what God said to Joseph and what was in the hearts of his brethren. Purely analogous to the struggle of The Church is idea of the lesser being more blessed of the better. Hebrews 7:7; The Office of the Apostle will release the Body of Christ into it's destiny. The anointing in the Office of The Apostle is necessary for the order and structure of the body. In this analogy then we find that the heart of God is the consummate key for understanding how God operates. The struggle of The Body of Christ is that Joseph is seen by his brethren; from the perspective of the flesh, and who he was in relationship to them. Their senses and emotions dictated their level of belief regarding his place (Joseph's) with them. They needed to see him as God saw him. The Church has judged one another and lived with their own expectation of what should be and not what the Living God has said regarding His Josephs. He does not choose us based on appearance or what we possess; nor does He consider us because of our astuteness, but it is our humility that provokes God in choosing us. It is the lack there of, which will cause us to be rejected. Joseph's brothers were full of pride and arrogance. *It is arrogant to dismiss what God has chosen!*

Let's consider the relationship between King Saul and God. Saul is very much rebellious against the order of God. God instructs him to go and destroy the Amalekites. The Amalekites are set by God for their destruction because of their hatred of Israel. Saul has done the thing that is arrogant and prideful in the eyes of God. It is arrogant in that Saul has not regarded the instruction of the Prophet Samuel to do everything that he was told to do. It is prideful in that Saul suggests to the Prophet that he has done everything that he was told to do, even though Saul has clearly done something different. This is because he believes that saving Agag alive and keeping the best cattle are more acceptable than God's plan to utterly destroy them. In 1st Samuel 15:17, Samuel said;

And Samuel said, When thou wast little in thine own sight, wast thou not made the head of the tribes of Israel, and the LORD anointed thee king over Israel? and the Lord anointed thee king over Israel? And the Lord sent thee on a journey, and said, Go and utterly destroy the sinners the Amalekites, and fight against them until they be consumed. Wherefore then didst thou not obey the voice of the Lord, but didst fly upon the spoil, and didst evil in the sight of the Lord? And Saul said unto Samuel, Yea, I have obeyed the voice of the Lord, and have gone the way, which the Lord sent me, and have brought Agag the king of Amalek, and have utterly destroyed the Amalekites. But the people took of the spoil, sheep and oxen, the chief of the things, which should have been utterly destroyed, to sacrifice unto the Lord thy God in Gilgal."

Like Saul, there is unwillingness in the people of God to accept responsibility for that which we have done. It is a breach of integrity in The Body of Christ against what we know to be true. Saul is willing to allow the blame for his rebellion to be cast to the people. While they are partly culpable; it is Saul who has been charged to utterly destroy the Amalekites and everything that they possessed. It is very prideful to dismiss the command of God and to input our own desires as though they were His intended will. No man can truly serve the Lord in his pride. God will reject pride! With this then we see a part of the struggle that exists in the Body of Christ. It is the need for headship and leadership to come into alignment with the Word of God. Because Saul did not align himself with the commanded will of the Lord; *(as headship)* those that followed him *(leadership)* were disobedient

and maintained their own agendas while leaving the perfect will of God for their pleasure.

1st Peter 5:5 tells us; "Likewise ye younger, submit yourselves unto the elder. Yea, all of you be subject one to another and be clothed with humility: for God resists the proud, and gives grace to the humble. Humble yourselves therefore under the mighty hand of God, that he may exalt you in due time."

How then can the Body of Christ submit to headship and leadership; when headship and leadership are not submitted to the authority of the God they are called to serve? God places great value on headship and it's obedience to His will. That which is done by headship and leadership impacts the fellowship of the saints. This then, is not unlike the error of Moses in smiting the rock in Numbers 20:10-12 and being judged by God for his disobedience. Note the heart of the Lord in showing Moses' rebellion.

"And Moses and Aaron gathered the congregation together before the Rock, and he said unto them, hear now, ye rebels; must we fetch you water out of this rock?

Vs. 11; And Moses lifted up his hand, and with his rod he smote the Rock twice: and the water came out abundantly, and the congregation drank, and their beasts also.

Vs. 12; And the Lord spoke unto Moses and Aaron, because ye believed me not, to sanctify me in the eyes of the Children of Israel, therefore ye shall not bring this congregation into the land which I have given them.

Moses not only knew the heart of the Lord but he had an obligation to sanctify Him in the presence of the people. Moses failed to do that and this was mirrored by his unbelief.
(Vs. 12) It would appear harsh but the fact of the matter is that Moses knew better and he was judged based on the relationship that he possessed with the Lord. He could not go over and possess the land of promise because of it. As with Saul, Moses is judged and rejected for his disobedience because he knew God's heart and had rejected it. In rejecting the heart of God; Moses showed his unbelief by failing to sanctify the Lord God before the

people. The headship ministry of the churches must be careful to sanctify the Lord God before the people of God in everything that God commands. Failure to do so is a breach of both ethical and moral responsibility. It would seem that there should be more grace for the flaws in Saul's character; as well as the temper tantrum of Moses; yet they had a willful disregard for the instruction the Lord had given them. With this statement there is some consideration that must be given to the issue of grace: the first being that of continuing in sin. While grace is a New Testament concept; it is not without merit in the Old Testament. In the Old Testament it is recognized in:

Proverbs 3:33-35; "The curse of the Lord is in the house of the wicked: but he blesses the habitation of the just.

Vs. 34; Surely he scorns the scorner, but he gives grace unto the lowly.

Vs 35; The wise shall inhabit glory but shame shall be the promotion of fools."

Saul was foolish and his end was shame. The Apostle Paul wrote to the Romans in:

Romans 6:1; "What shall we say then? Shall we continue in sin, that grace may abound?"

There is principally, a demonstration of unbalance in the Body of Christ at times, because of the willingness to blatantly operate in sin. It is a lack of regard; for the truth as commanded in our obedience. We then, promote folly because of our sins. Conversely, it brings the Body of Christ into an imbalance, not understanding that we must operate in grace and the fear of the Lord.

Acts 9:31; "then had the churches rest throughout all Judea and Galilee and Samaria, and were edified; and walking in the fear of the Lord and in the comfort of the Holy Ghost, were multiplied"

The fear of the Lord keeps hearts and minds from willful sin. This is the aspect of maturity in the believer and in the Body of Christ that allows for

the making of judicious decisions which show Christ as sovereign. The comfort of the Holy Spirit is the grace that is given in our frailty, which then removes the guilt and condemnation that would otherwise keep us bound and broken in our failures.

1 John 1:9 tells us; "My little children, these things write I unto you, THAT YE SIN NOT. If any man sin, we have an advocate with the Father, Jesus Christ the righteous."

The Body of Christ must have balance. Joseph did not choose himself; God did. It is clearly seen in the humility of Joseph, as he walked out his struggle. Then God elevated him as the Apostolic headship over his brethren. Many will live beneath their purpose and miss their destiny because they live in the flesh. The mandate of the Spirit of Christ is one of agreement with God's purpose and will. The Church has at times been walking in a Pseudo-Christian relationship. It has not truly known Him!

"For who has known the mind of the Lord, that he may instruct him? But we have the mind of Christ." 1st Cor. 2:16

Therefore, the people of the Lord must know Him and have His heart and mind to do that which is pleasing according to His will. The heart of the Father is revealed in His Son. Jesus Christ is the key to knowing the Father. The Church has been very sluggish and resistant to the will of God. There are those divisions and strife, which beset the Body; along with envies and confusion. At times, there is total disregard for the price paid by Him, to bring men into agreement. It is a price that we as men could not pay. How can we then, not obey the Spirit of God and walk in His order? How then does this tie us to the need to gather Benjamin into the Kingdom of God? It is firstly, the aspect of the prophetic pronouncement of Jacob before he is gathered to his fathers. In Genesis 49:27 it says;

"Benjamin shall ravin as a wolf: in the morning he shall devour the prey, and at night he shall divide the spoil."

This is a tremendous look at the nature and character of Benjamin. He is a warrior and fighter and is very distinctive in his perception and discerning. He, in the Spirit Realm, is one who will know what it is to be sincere and genuine in the intentions of the heart. He will not be easily or readily fooled. Benjamin will be a warring and aggressive end time people. They will be as is referred to in: Matthew 11:12;

"and from the days of John the Baptist until now, the kingdom of heaven suffers violence, and the violent take it by force."

Note that it is yet, the teaching of the Apostles heart to this generation that will bring equipping, instruction and order to their lives. his Fathering Spirit was released in John the Baptist as noted in Malachi 4:5-6. Therefore, the spirit of the Body of Christ will be that of Benjamin the Warrior in this end time. It will be the boldness and aggressiveness of the younger generations of this world to come into the Kingdom of God and fight through the strongholds of a vicious adversary and establish the Sons of God in the earth. This is the manifestation that all creation is travailing for. Rom. 8:19-22

The Church is being pressed upon by the Spirit of God to seek out the lost and broken and wounded of the earth. However, there is a great thrust in the Body of Christ to bring the youth of our generations into right relationship with God. They will not walk in the failures of their fathers and neither will they live in hypocrisy. They will be a generation that is full of integrity and submitted to the will of Christ without ambiguities. That is to say that they will be completely sold out for the Kingdom of God's sake. Let us look then parenthetically at the history of Benjamin and the pressure of warfare the enemy had determined against them. In the book of Judges the 20th chapter we find the near eradication of Benjamin. It is a time when they were very valorous and dedicated to people. In this regard they were much like the gangs of this nation for commitment and steadfastness. That is, they were very determined to win in battle even when fighting for the wrong causes. Let's look at Judges 19:22-30; as a very clear parallel is made in regard to the zeal and strength of Benjamin in battle.

This is the time recorded in the Word of God, where a Levite goes to the city of Gibeah, which is in Benjamin. He is going from Bethlehem–Judah to the house of the Lord and is received by an old man of Mount Ephraim into his house. The Levite received straw and provender for his ass, and they washed their feet and did eat and drink. (Vs.21) Then some sons of Belial came according to scripture and surrounded the house. They came with the idea of committing acts of lasciviousness against the Levite. The old man convinced them to take the concubine of the Levite and his daughter instead. They took his concubine and abused her all night long. This is the wickedness of the hearts of men, first; to desire the flesh of other men and because they could not have it, abuse and murder his concubine. It is an abomination to Israel. Note: This is also a particular abomination in this nation as well. The spirit of sodomy and lewdness is in full force in our country and God is not pleased with the willingness to accept such aberrant behavior by our communities. Now, in the Church there is a cry for the righteousness of God to become the standard for the entirety of the Body of Christ. Israel represents the Body of Christ. Here then is the struggle for the Church. That is; a focused commitment to destroying the works of the flesh which hinder the presence and power of God from bringing an active demonstration of Jesus Christ into the Body with constancy. This has not happened because we; the Body of Christ, have not agreed continually with the Holy Ghost. There is an insistence of the Spirit of God for obedience and continual submission to Him. Until the Church complies with the Word of God by conduct and proper intent of its spirit: it cannot receive God's fullness. This can only be born out through the Spirit of Elijah. See Mal. 4:5-6. This is the Fathering heart of God to bring God's people into proper relationship with God. It must start with proper headship and then flow through the Body of Christ. Jesus asks a question in Luke 11:9-13. He starts off by saying in verse 9;

"and I say unto you, ask and it shall be given to you; seek, and ye shall find; knock, and it shall be opened unto you.

Vs 10; For everyone that asks, receives; and he that seeks, finds; and to him that knocks, it shall be opened.

Vs. 11; If a son shall ask bread of any of you that is a father, will he give him a stone? Or if he ask a fish, will he for a
fish give him a serpent?

Vs 12; Or if he shall ask an egg, will he offer him a scorpion?

Vs 13; If ye then, being evil know how to give good gifts unto your children; how much more shall your heavenly Father give the Holy Spirit to them that ask him?"

The ministry of headship must seek after the wisdom and heart of the Father for the ability to impact the kingdom of God for Christ's sake. Parts of the Body of Christ are suffering a type of death because of what has been allowed to come into the Church. It is sin which causes festering and spiritual death, without any true standard of holiness; that confronts and challenges these sins. There are such issues as, homosexuality and lesbianism that have become acceptable to the Church and without the proper standard of righteousness, will remain, as a part of the norm for many ministries. This was a theme in the history of Israel that is seen throughout the scripture. The men of Gibeah were no different from those that were in Sodom and Gomorrah. Now because of the flagrant sin of these individuals the whole of Israel is offended and wounded by their abominations. The Levites concubine died. She then, is cut up into little pieces and sent throughout Israel which incites the fury of the tribes of Israel against the men of Gibeah. Gibeah of course is a city in the borders of Benjamin. When asked by Israel to give them the men of that city who did these atrocious acts, there was great resistance. The context of the Word of God here is one of extreme importance. There is in many instances a need to purge the land of the sin and to bring all things to righteousness. Now again we do not say these things to condemn anyone but to say that sin in any form can only be challenged and defeated with the truth of God's Word. It is the standard of truth that challenges and destroys sin in the heart. When the heart is changed, men will do what is right in the eyes of Christ. That in the vale of this writing; we speak to the issues of men being accountable to call sin sin, even when it means the loss of that which we love and esteem as a part of our own. This was such a blatant and infuriating refusal on the part of the men of Gibeah, that it nearly destroyed the entire tribe of Benjamin. God

is not opposed to the calling for of judgment against the sins of men even in the civil affairs of man. How much more will He expect the executions of righteousness against the sin of the wicked? This points out the extreme necessity for the sin of the wicked? This points out the extreme necessity for the Apostolic graces in the Body of Christ. It is the call for the order of God to the affairs of the Church and a greater accountability for the actions of the Body of Christ. It is a revealing of the nature and the character of the Father and His attributes. This unveiling ministers the heart of God and establishes the image of His son in the Church. The accountability for sin and the willingness to be conformed to His image in every area of our living becomes the focus of the Christ of heaven. That is to establish His kingdom in us. Joseph then is a living example of the Apostolic grace and the willingness to bring healing to the whole body. He walks in righteousness in his living and through all that he is faced with. He looks to reconcile his family even though he has been wronged by his brothers and suffered many things for the sake of the purposes of the Kingdom of God.

The final concern for Joseph is one of the bringing of his brother Benjamin into Egypt to stand before him and to be reconciled with him. Benjamin is a very important key to the purposes of the Kingdom because of his warring mentality. His destiny is one of vanquisher of the enemies of the Lord. He stands beside Judah as a warrior in the affairs of the Kingdom and stabilizes the southern kingdom. Too many times the enemy of our soul has gained an occasion against us because we have failed to judge our own sins and have them covered through the blood of Christ through confession and repentance for sin. The Church must recognize that its destiny is tied to the total and complete righteousness of Christ in every area of our living. Nothing can be hidden or held back. When we do not live in the obedience of Christ; we negate the effectiveness of the Body to perform the whole will of Christ. We also, negate the potential for becoming everything that we were born to become in life. All of creation is groaning and travailing until now, waiting for the manifestations of the Sons of God.

Finally, Joseph after having been reconciled to his brothers is reunited with his father and the illustrious history of an entire nation is born out of the reconciliation and healing that came to this family. What a glorious vision of God's provision for us, in that Body of Christ can be healed through Christ's love and forgiveness. Joseph as a type and shadow of Christ in the midst of his persecution and suffering, gives himself to God's plan for his life and is then able to forgive his brothers and be restored to relationship with them and also to be restored in fellowship with his father. God's desire for us shows the quality of HIS love and grace to every believer. That is, we walk as he walks and do the things that HE does. We can then see our generations filled with HIS heart and love through our obedience to God's Word. The word of the Lord is fulfilled: In Isaac shall thy seed be blessed. How magnanimous is the Word of God to establish His promises and bring Israel to the world. We find now, that the Lord is yet fulfilling His word and establishing His promises with His people. So shall it be in this end time as a more declarative word is pronounced in the midst of the people of God. It is the word of faith that cannot be denied and the Body of Christ will be fully revealed in the Word of truth. It's time to go get Benjamin!!

About the Author

Biography: Apostle William O. Epps Jr

Apostle Epps is the eldest of eight children born to William and Katherine Epps. Apostle Epps was born again in November of 1975. He was called to preach 9 months later and has been in ministry for 35 years. He was then called as a Teacher and Evangelist in the first 18 years of his ministry serving under Pastor Preston Kelker for 7 years at Grace Temple Revivals. After that time He served under Apostle Earl Thomas for another 3 years before being sent by the Lord to San Diego, Ca where he served in various capacities under Pastor Vernon Cooper Jr. Apostle Epps was there for 10 years before God called him to the Pastoral ministry. He then became Pastor of Deliverance Tabernacle Church in Akron, Ohio in 1994. During that time he learned about the prophet call and Apostolic office on his life. Since that time he has co-founded The International Council of Apostles and Prophets with Apostle Earl Thomas of Community Fellowship Church in Akron, Ohio. (ICAP) is a ministry that serves to work with ministries of similar heart and vision for the transformation and establishing of the Body of Christ in the perfect will and design of Christ for this time. He has written 3 books . He is married to his wife Carolyn and has 10 children. Apostle Epps still serves now, as the Pastor of New & Living Way Ministries in Akron, Ohio in addition to His extensive travel and ministry to the Body of Christ.

Printed in the United States
By Bookmasters